QUESTIONS AND ANSWERS

WILD WILD WORLD

This is a Parragon Publishing book
This edition published in 2005

Parragon Publishing
Queen Street House
4 Queen Street
Bath BA1 1HE, UK

Copyright © Parragon 2001

British Library Cataloguing-in-Publication Data

A catalogue record for this book is available from the British Library.

ISBN 1-40545-813-5

Printed in China

Originally produced by David West Children's Books
This edition by Design Principals

Illustrators James Field Sarah Lees Terry Riley Ross Watton (SGA) Rob Shone
Cartoonist Peter Wilks (SGA)
Editor James Pickering *Consultant* Steve Parker

QUESTIONS AND ANSWERS
WILD WILD WORLD

Written by

Anita Ganeri

Clare Oliver

Denny Robson

Contents

CHAPTER THREE
SNAKES AND OTHER REPTILES

CHAPTER FOUR
SHARKS AND OTHER DANGEROUS FISH

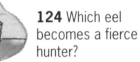

173 Who hides a feast in the trees?

174 How can you tell small cats from big?

174 Which cat barks?

175 Which cat has the most kittens?

176 Do hyenas laugh?

177 Do hyena cubs get on together?

177 Do hyenas hunt?

178 How do dogs hunt?

178 Do dogs use babysitters?

179 What do pups eat?

180 What changes its coat in the winter?

180 Who's at home in the city?

181 Who won the race, the fox or the hare?

182 Which is the biggest dog?

183 Do wolves howl at the Moon?

183 Which wolf walks on stilts?

184 Which is the biggest bear?

185 Which cubs drink the creamiest milk?

185 Can bears walk on water?

186 Which bear fishes for its supper?

186 When do bears climb trees?

187 Do all bears eat meat?

188 Where can you see bears close-up?

189 How do dogs help people?

189 Where can you see big cats close-up?

CHAPTER SEVEN
WHALES AND OTHER SEA MAMMALS

192 What are sea mammals?

193 Which special features help whales live in the sea?

193 Which is the biggest sea mammal?

194 Do all whales have teeth?

195 What has tiny shellfish on its back?

195 What's the difference between whales and dolphins?

196 What do walruses use their tusks for?

196 Which seal blows up balloons?

197 Which seals live at the ends of the Earth?

198 Where do manatees and dugongs live?

199 How can you tell manatees and dugongs apart?

199 Which sea mammals are vegetarians?

200 Which sea mammal can swim the fastest?

201 Which is the speediest seal?

201 What is one of the deepest divers?

202 Which whales turn somersaults in the air?

202 Which sea mammals walk with their teeth?

203 Which sea mammals make the longest journey?

204 Which are the most intelligent sea mammals?

204 Which seal has a huge nose?

205 Why do whales sing to each other?

206 Which whale has the longest 'teeth'?

206 How do leopard seals catch their prey?

207 Which sea mammal has the biggest appetite?

208 What finds food with its whiskers?

208 Which sea mammals use fishing nets?

209 What uses a ceiling of water to catch fish?

210 How can you tell humpback whales apart?

211 Why are killer whales black and white?

211 Which whales change color as they grow up?

212 Which are the biggest sea mammal babies?

212 Which sea mammals live in a pod?

213 Which sea mammals live the longest?

CHAPTER EIGHT
GORILLAS AND OTHER PRIMATES

CHAPTER ONE

DINOSAURS

AND OTHER PREHISTORIC REPTILES

What were the dinosaurs?

Dinosaurs were reptiles of many amazing shapes and sizes that lived long ago. They had just the same needs as the animals you know today – to hunt, feed, breed and escape their enemies.

Herrerasaurus

Triassic   Jurassic

Is it true?

Dinosaurs only lived on land.

YES. They were adapted for life on land because they walked with straight legs tucked underneath their bodies, as we do. This gave them an advantage over other animals and helped them dominate the land.

Cretaceous

Where did they live?

Everywhere on Earth, but the planet was completely different in dinosaur times. The seas, plants, animals and continents, Laurasia and Gondwana, were all different. And there were no people!

Laurasia

Gondwana

When did they live?

Dinosaurs ruled the world for millions of years. They appeared about 225 million years ago and died out 65 million years ago. There were three periods in dinosaur history: Triassic, when the first dinosaurs appeared; Jurassic and Cretaceous, when dinosaurs dominated the land.

Amazing! One of the earliest dinosaurs ever found was Eoraptor, 'dawn stealer', and it lived 225 million years ago. It was only three feet long and probably a fierce hunter of small reptiles.

Eoraptor

? Were there any other animals?

Insects, small mammals and many modern forms of life lived in the shadow of the dinosaurs, as well as other reptiles. Pterosaurs soared through the air, while ichthyosaurs and plesiosaurs swam in the seas.

Pterosaurs

Plesiosaur

Ichthyosaur

? Where did dinosaurs come from?

There was life on Earth for over 3,000 million years before the dinosaurs. Mammal-like reptiles were living on the land just before the dinosaurs appeared. Some scientists think Lagosuchus (which means rabbit crocodile) was the ancestor of all dinosaurs.

Lagosuchus

Amazing! There were many groups of land-based reptiles 245 million years ago. These included crocodile-like animals which grew up to 17 feet long.

Archaeopteryx

How do we know that dinosaurs existed?

Scientists called paleontologists examine dinosaur bones and piece them together. They also study fossilized footprints, nests and eggs, dung and even toothmarks on bones.

Fossils

Lizard

Deltatheridium

Is it true?
We know everything about dinosaurs from fossils.

NO. Scientists must guess what color dinosaurs were, what noises they made and how they behaved. They compare what they know about dinosaurs with the animals alive today.

Hesperorni

? Which were the biggest dinosaurs?

In the Jurassic age, giant plant eaters called sauropods became the largest animals to walk on Earth. One of them, Ultrasauros, may have been up to 100 feet long and about 60 feet high, which is as tall as a six-story building!

 Is it true?
All sauropods were huge and wide.

NO. Sauropods were huge, but some were 'slim'. This helped when they walked through woods looking for food.

Compsognathus

? Which were the smallest dinosaurs?

Compsognathus was the size of a turkey and weighed about six pounds. It hunted insects and lizards. Heterodontosaurus and Lesothosaurus, both plant-eating dinosaurs, were just as small.

Which were the heaviest dinosaurs?
Ultrasauros may have weighed as much as 50 tons, but scientists have recently found evidence of an even bigger dinosaur in Argentina. The gigantic Argentinosaurus may have weighed as much as 100 tons. Most sauropods were smaller, weighing between 30 and 80 tons.

Ultrasauros

Amazing! The neck of Mamenchisaurus was 50 feet long, strengthened by a system of spines. It could not have been lifted very high. Mamenchisaurus probably fed on low-growing vegetation.

How do we know which dinosaurs ate meat, and which ate plants?

We can tell by looking at fossils of their teeth and claws. Meat eaters and plant eaters developed different special features, such as hands that could grasp and grinding or shearing teeth.

Plant eater fossil

Meat eater fossil

Yunnanosaurus

What were plant eaters' teeth like?

Yunnanosaurus had chisel-like teeth to cut up tough vegetation. Some sauropods had spoon-shaped teeth for cutting tough plants. Diplodocids had pencil-shaped teeth. They could strip branches bare in seconds by raking leaves through their teeth.

What were meat eaters' teeth and claws like?

Meat eaters such as Allosaurus had long, curved, dagger-like teeth to kill and tear at prey. They had powerful jaws in their large heads and strong claws to grip their victims. Allosaurus could eat you up in two gulps!

Allosaurus

 Is it true?
Some dinosaurs ate stones.

Yes. Plant eaters swallowed stones called gastroliths, to help grind down tough plant food inside their stomachs. Gastroliths were up to four inches across.

Amazing!
Carcharodontosaurus had a huge skull five feet across, with jaws full of teeth like a shark's. And yet some dinosaurs had no teeth at all! Gallimimus fed mainly on insects and tiny creatures it could swallow whole.

Tyrannosaurus rex

Whose teeth were as long as knives?

Tyrannosaurus rex, one of the last dinosaurs, was also one of the largest and fiercest meat eaters ever to live on Earth. Its ferocious teeth were six inches long. It used them to strip away flesh while it held its prey down with its feet.

Tenontosaurus

Is it true?
Some dinosaurs were cannibals.

Yes. Two skeletons of Coelophysis have been found containing the bones of smaller Coelophysis. They had eaten the young animals as their last meal.

What would kick out at its prey?

Deinonychus had an enormous slashing claw on each foot. It probably hunted and killed in packs, attacking its prey with a flying leap.

Baryonyx

Deinonychus

Amazing!

Baryonyx had large, curved claws that may have been used for hooking fish out of water. Its jaw was very similar to the jaws of modern fish-eating crocodiles.

What had a 'terrible hand'?

Deinocheirus means 'terrible hand'. It had hands with long claws which must have been deadly, and arms ten feet long. Compared to this, T. rex's arms were tiny!

❓ What used its tongue in the same way as a giraffe?

Iguanodon used its long tongue to pull leaves into its mouth. On the 'thumb' of each hand it had a defensive spike. When this was first discovered, people thought it was a horn from its nose!

Iguanodon

Brachiosaurus

🖼 Is it true?
Most dinosaurs were peaceful, plant-eating creatures which never attacked anything.

Yes. Most dinosaurs were actually gentle animals, rather than monster killing machines like Tyrannosaurus Rex.

❓ Which dinosaurs traveled in groups?

Fossilized footprints from 80 million years ago tell us that Brachiosaurus traveled in herds, like most other plant-eating sauropods. It had huge nostrils, perhaps to smell with, to help cool it, or even to make a noise.

Amazing! Huge plant eaters had to eat a huge amount. A Brachiosaurus may have eaten a ton of vegetation a day. It must have spent its whole day walking, eating and producing waste!

Psittacosaurus

What had a beak like a parrot?

Psittacosaurus means 'parrot reptile'. With a narrow, parrot-like beak, strong jaws and sharp teeth, it was able to chew through very tough plants.

Were huge plant eaters ever attacked?

The sheer size of many of these gentle giants must have put off many predators. Some like Apatosaurus had long claws to defend themselves in case they were attacked. They would rear up on their back legs and slash out at their enemies.

Heterodontosaurus

Ceratosaurus

 Amazing! Plant eaters like Heterodontosaurus had fangs which they may have used to bite attackers. It was a small but strong dinosaur, well able to defend itself against meat eaters.

 Is it true? Scientists can tell how quickly dinosaurs could travel.

YES. By looking at their skeletons and measuring the distance between fossilized footprints, scientists can measure how quickly or slowly a dinosaur moved.

Apatosaurus

? What had spikes at the end of its tail?

The enemies of Stegosaurus would have had to watch out for the bony spikes in its tail. Many plant-eating dinosaurs developed spikes, horns or claws to protect themselves from attack.

? What could run away from attackers?

Some small plant eaters relied on running away to defend themselves. They would have had good hearing and sharp eyesight. Dryosaurus could run at about 25 mph.

Dryosaurus

25

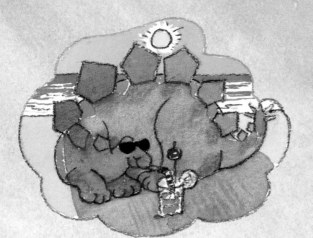

What whacked its enemies with a club?

The skull and body of Euoplocephalus were protected with bony plates, spines and spikes. It also had a huge club at the end of its tail. When attacked, it would swing this club at its enemy.

Is it true?
Stegosaurus used the plates on its back to defend itself.

NO. The plates may have looked frightening to enemies. But it's more likely that they helped control the animal's body temperature, so that it could warm up and cool down when it needed to.

Hylaeosaurus

Euoplocephalus

What wore armor to protect itself?

Many dinosaurs had a thick layer of bony skin which protected them like a suit of armor. Hylaeosaurus would lie low to the ground so that its attacker couldn't get under its armor.

Amazing! Another armored dinosaur, Huayangosaurus, had sharp spikes running from its shoulder to the middle of its tail. When it was attacked, it would point the spikes on its back at the enemy and lash out with its tail.

Tyrannosaurus rex

Triceratops

What had a horn like a rhinoceros?

Triceratops had three large horns, two over its eyes and one on its snout. Its neck and shoulders were protected by a frill of bone. There were many horned dinosaurs, most of which fed together in herds.

Which dinosaurs had 'trumpets'?

Many 'duck-billed' dinosaurs, like Parasaurolophus, had strange crests on their heads. The male's crest was much larger than the female's. It was hollow and connected to the nostrils. Perhaps these dinosaurs used their crests like trumpets, making sounds to show off to their mates or to threaten rival males.

 Is it true?
Scientists were the first people to discover dinosaur tracks.

NO. Native Americans were using designs which included dinosaur footprints, long before dinosaur tracks were discovered by scientists.

Parasaurolophus

Pachycephalosaurus

Diplodocus

Allosaurus

What used its tail as a whip?

Diplodocus was a huge, plant-eating dinosaur with an enormously long neck and tail. It could measure 88 feet from nose to tail. When it was attacked, it used its tail like a whip, lashing it from side to side.

What used to fight with its head?

Male dinosaurs probably fought for territory and mates, like animals do today. Pachycephalosaurus had a skull with a dome of thick bone, like a crash helmet. This was probably to protect its brain during head-butting fights with rivals.

Did dinosaurs lay eggs?

Yes. Dinosaurs laid eggs, just as reptiles and birds do today. Scientists have found fossil eggs all over the world. Most are empty, but some eggs have been found with the fossil bones of baby dinosaurs inside.

Centrosaurus

Did dinosaurs protect their young?

Horned dinosaurs like Centrosaurus lived in large family groups, like elephants. When threatened, the adults probably surrounded the young, making a frightening wall of horns.

Amazing! Oviraptor was thought to live on stolen eggs, because its skeleton was found on the eggs of another dinosaur. But a baby Oviraptor has now been found inside one of the eggs. So scientists can't decide if it's a thief or not!

Maiasaura

Is it true?
Dinosaur eggs were huge.

NO. Dinosaur eggs were only about 5 inches long. If they were bigger, the shell would have been too thick for the young to break through.

? Which reptile made nests?

Maiasaura, 'good mother reptile', made nests in groups. Each parent would dig a hollow in the sand, the female would lay up to 25 eggs, then the eggs were covered with plants to keep them warm.

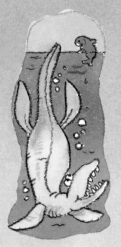

Amazing! The largest lizards ever were mosasaurs, huge reptiles that swam in the sea. They were real sea monsters – 32 feet long with huge mouths, and they looked like dragons! They probably ate anything they could catch.

Were there dinosaurs in the sea?

No. All dinosaurs lived on land, but there was a variety of strange reptiles that swam in the seas in dinosaur times. Ichthyosaurs were strong swimming reptiles that looked like dolphins and could breathe air. They probably hunted in packs, feeding on fish and squid.

Ammonite

Ichthyosaurs

Is it true?
The Loch Ness Monster exists.

WHO KNOWS? People who believe that there really is a monster in Loch Ness in Scotland, think it may well be a plesiosaur. What do you think?

What was all neck?

Plesiosaurs were also swimming reptiles. They had four paddle-like limbs and a tail. Elasmosaurus was a long-necked plesiosaur. Its tiny head sat on an amazingly long neck that was half its total length of 42 feet.

Elasmosaurus

Liopleurodon

What had a huge head?

Liopleurodon was one of the short-necked plesiosaurs. But its head was twelve feet long! It probably fed on shellfish and turtles, crunching them up with dagger-like teeth that were four inches long.

33

Archaeopteryx

❓ What was the earliest bird?

The earliest bird discovered was Archaeopteryx, which lived 150 million years ago. Birds are the dinosaurs' closest living relatives. Some scientists believe they evolved from dinosaurs such as Deinonychus, only smaller.

Amazing!

Pterodaustro had a sieve in its beak so that it could strain fish from the water as it flew low over the sea.

Rhamphorhynchus

❓ Were there flying dinosaurs?

The reptiles gliding through the air weren't dinosaurs but pterosaurs. The earliest pterosaurs were rhamphorhynchids which appeared about 200 million years ago.

What were pterodactyls?

Pterodactyls, which means 'wing-finger', were pterosaurs. They were sleek and streamlined, and grew to huge sizes. They had crests on their heads, but no tail and no teeth. They appeared 150 million years ago and died out at the same time as the dinosaurs.

Pterodactylus

Is it true?

Quetzalcoatlus was bigger than a hang-glider.

YES. This huge pterodactyl was the biggest airborne animal that ever lived. It had a wingspan of up to 50 feet.

? Why did the dinosaurs disappear?

Some scientists think it was because a large meteorite hit Earth, or because huge volcanoes erupted and the climate changed. Movement of land and seas meant there were also fewer places for dinosaurs to live. It could be all of these reasons.

Amazing! A huge crater 110 miles across has been found on the seabed near Mexico. It was formed 65 million years ago. Could this be from a meteorite that wiped out the dinosaurs?

? Why would a meteorite wipe out the dinosaurs?

When the meteorite hit the surface of the Earth, there would have been a huge explosion. Dust would fill the air, blocking out the Sun's light for several months. Without the Sun vegetation would die, the plant eaters would die, and finally the large meat eaters would starve.

Zalambdalestes

Is it true?

People may have caused dinosaurs to become extinct.

NO. People and dinosaurs have never lived at the same time. There is a 50 million year gap between the last dinosaurs and the first human beings. So don't believe all the films that you see!

Did all the animals disappear?

No, although many other species died out along with the dinosaurs. These included pterosaurs and marine reptiles such as plesiosaurs. Most bigger animals became extinct. But smaller animals survived, and these creatures evolved in a world without the dinosaur.

How do museums make dinosaur skeletons?

Lots of people are involved, from fossil hunters to people who transport the bones, paleontologists, laboratory technicians, even artists and photographers. The bones are put together in order and held in place by steel supports.

Is it true?
Artists can help to show what dinosaurs looked like.

YES. When scientists have identified bones, artists draw what the dinosaur might have looked like when it was alive.

Do museums use real bones?

No. Original fossils are too heavy and valuable. Instead scientists make copies from lightweight materials and keep the real bones safe.

STAFF ONLY

DINO DETOUR

 Amazing! Scientists think that they might have found a missing link between birds and dinosaurs. Sinosauropteryx was a true dinosaur, but it had a feathery covering, and its feet had sharp pointed claws, much like a chicken's.

Sinosauropteryx

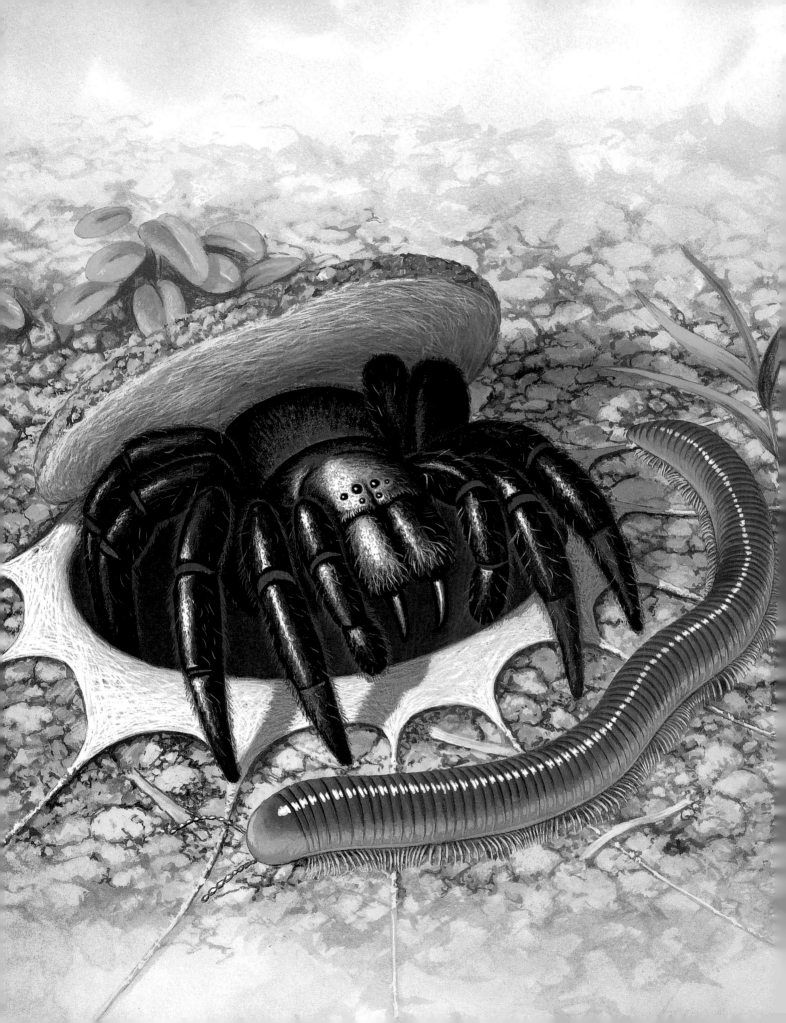

CHAPTER TWO

SPIDERS

AND OTHER CREEPY-CRAWLIES

Are spiders insects?

No. Spiders belong to a group called arachnids, which also includes scorpions, mites and ticks. Spiders all have eight legs, one pair more than insects. They have two body parts – a head and an abdomen – and most have eight simple eyes.

Is it true?
Spiders and insects have bones.

NO. Instead they all have a hard casing on the outside called an exoskeleton. This protects their soft insides like a suit of armor and gives them their shape. They have to replace this casing with a new one in order to grow.

Wolf spider

Amazing! There are creepy-crawlies living just about everywhere in the world, underwater, in caves, down deep holes and even on the tops of mountains. Most of the animals in the world are insects. They make up 85% of all known animal species and there are probably millions more waiting to be discovered!

Head

Thorax

Abdomen

❓ What makes an insect an insect?

Although they may look different from one another, every adult insect has six legs and three parts to its body. The head is at the front, the thorax in the middle and the abdomen at the back. Many insects have wings for flying and long feelers or antennae.

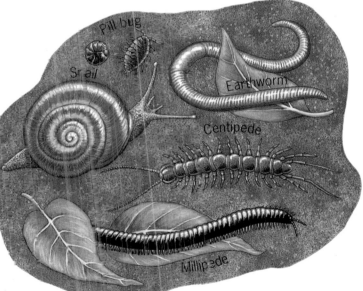

Pill bug

Snail

Earthworm

Centipede

Millipede

❓ What is a minibeast?

Creepy-crawlies can also be called minibeasts. You will find other kinds of minibeasts in this book which are related to spiders and insects, such as Pill bugs, slugs, snails, worms, centipedes and millipedes.

Which insect is as heavy as an apple?

The heaviest insect in the world is the African Goliath beetle. It weighs about four ounces and can be six inches long. It lives in rotten wood in tropical forests.

Is it true?
Some creepy-crawlies can live for 50 years.

YES. A queen termite may live to this ripe old age. But the life of an adult mayfly may be only a few hours long – just enough time for the mayfly to find a mate.

Goliath beetle

What grows up inside the eggs of other insects?

Fairy flies are actually tiny wasps, some of which have a wing span no bigger than a period! The female can lay up to 20 eggs inside the egg of another insect.

Fairy fly on insect eggs

Amazing! Fleas can jump 150 times their own body length. If humans could do this, we would be able to jump a third of a mile in the air! Fleas are wingless insects which suck blood from birds and mammals.

Rhinoceros beetle

Which is the strongest creature in the world?

Believe it or not, it's an insect. The rhinoceros beetle is able to move 850 times its own weight. Can you imagine trying to carry 850 people the same size as you?

❓ Do spiders have teeth?

No, but they have fangs for stabbing prey and injecting it with poison and special juices. The victims turn to liquid inside so that the spider can then suck them up like soup!

Indian ornamental tarantula

❓ Why do spiders spin webs?

Sticky webs can be a home and a trap to catch flying insects. But not all spiders make webs, and not all webs are the same. The ogre-eyed spider makes a web like a net. It hangs down holding the web, waiting to throw it over its prey.

What can see with its tail?

As well as a sting, some scorpions also have light-sensitive cells in their tails. These cells let them know whether it's day or night, even when their heads are underground. Scorpions hunt at night and spend the day hidden in their burrows.

Emperor scorpion

Is it true?
Some spiders eat their webs.

YES. Orb web spiders eat the old web before they spin a new one. A web may take an hour to spin. The silk is as strong as steel of the same thickness.

Amazing! The water spider makes its home under the surface of the water. It spins a web like a balloon which it fills with air bubbles. It waits inside until it spots its prey, and then darts out to seize it.

Water spider

What can find its mate over a mile away in the dark?

Using its enormous feathery antennae, the male emperor moth can track down the scent of its mate even when she is far away. An insect's antennae are used for touching, smelling and tasting.

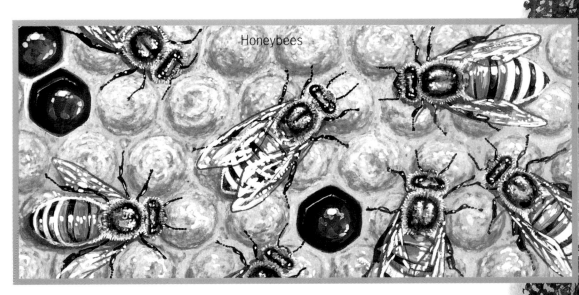
Honeybees

What does the waggle dance?

When a honeybee finds a good source of nectar, it flies back to the hive and does a special dance. The speed and direction of its movements tell the others where they can find the nectar.

Is it true?
All beetles can fly.

NO. Most have wings, but not all can fly. Beetles usually have two sets of wings. The first set is hard and strong, with the flying wings hidden beneath.

48

Eyes of a fly

Emperor moth

? Why is it so hard to swat a fly?

An insect's eye is made up of thousands of lenses. This means it sees a very different world from us. It's also much better at sensing any movement nearby.

Amazing! Dragonflies and some wasps and moths can fly as fast as 30 mph. Butterflies flap their wings 5 – 12 times per second, the hawkmoth 70 times, while some tiny flies can beat their wings 1,000 times each second!

What is the difference between a centipede and a millipede?

Centipedes and millipedes have long, bendy bodies made up of segments. A millipede has two pairs of legs on each segment, but centipedes have only one pair on each segment. Millipedes are plant eaters. Centipedes are meat eaters, hunting at night for tiny creatures which they attack with powerful poisonous jaws.

Snail

Centipede

What travels on one big foot?

Snails and slugs glide slowly along on one long muscular foot, leaving a trail of slime behind them. They prefer damp, dark places and are most active at night.

Is it true?

It's a bad thing to have worms in your garden.

NO. Gardeners like worms. Earthworms feed on dead plants and soil. As they move through the earth they help mix the soil, which is good. Their burrows put air in the soil and help water to drain away.

? How do worms move?

Earthworms live in burrows in the ground. They have no legs, no feet and no skeleton. But their long soft bodies are perfectly shaped to move easily through the earth. They move by stretching and contracting their muscles.

Earthworms

Millipede

Amazing! There are some giant creepy-crawlies. Giant worms in Australia can reach over six feet in length. Some centipedes and millipedes can reach a foot in length. And the largest land snail, the giant African land snail, is a monster compared with the common garden snail!

❓ What is the difference between a moth and a butterfly?

Butterflies are often brightly colored. They fly during the day and their antennae have rounded ends. Moths have feathery antennae, and fly at night.

Croesus moth

Heliconid butterfly

❓ Which butterfly can fly thousands of miles?

The American monarch butterfly lives in the United States and Canada. When autumn approaches, thousands travel south to Florida, California and Mexico – a journey of over 1,800 miles.

Peacock butterfly

Is it true?
Butterflies and moths have scales.

YES. Butterflies and moths have four wings covered with tiny overlapping scales which shimmer in the light. These scales give them their bold patterns and beautiful colors.

Amazing! Before laying eggs, butterflies test food plants with their antennae and tongues to check that the leaves are suitable for their caterpillars. But some also stamp on the leaves, because butterflies, flies and honeybees have taste organs in their feet!

Metamorphosis

How do caterpillars become butterflies?

When a caterpillar is fully grown, it turns into a pupa. Inside the pupa case the caterpillar's body breaks down and gradually becomes a butterfly. This change is called metamorphosis.

Tortoiseshell butterfly

53

When is a plant not a plant?

When it's a stick or leaf insect! Stick and leaf insects are the same color and shape as the twigs and leaves on which they feed. During the day they sit very still. Predators leave them alone because they don't realize that they are insects.

Eyed hawkmoth

Leaf insect

Stick insect

What frightens off enemies with its 'eyes'?

The eyed hawkmoth raises its front wings to show bold markings which look like large eyes. This fools enemies into thinking the moth is a much bigger animal than it really is.

54

Amazing! Beetles and pill bugs have an armor covering so tough that it is difficult to crush. This protects them from their enemies. Some pill bugs and millipedes roll into a ball like a hedgehog when they are threatened.

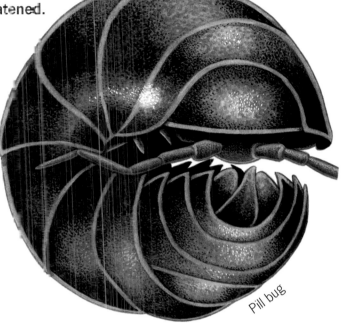

Pill bug

What pretends to be dead?

Click beetles lie on their backs as if they were dead to fool their enemies. Then they suddenly spring up in the air, twist and land on their feet, and run away!

Is it true?

Some spiders can change color.

YES. Crab spiders can change color to match the flowers they hide in. Lots of insects use camouflage to hide from their enemies. Invisible against the petals, the crab spider can pounce on unsuspecting bees, flies and butterflies as they visit the flower.

What uses a lasso to catch its prey?

The Bolas spider gives off a scent that attracts a particular moth. When the moth approaches, the spider swings out a line of silk with a sticky ball at the end. The ball sticks to the moth. The spider then hauls it in for supper.

Bolas spider

Stag beetles

 Amazing! Some insects' jaws have become weapons. Beetles have strong biting jaws. The largest belong to the stag beetle. They look like antlers and can be as long as the beetle's body. Beetles are the largest group of animals in the world, with over 300,000 kinds!

What is well equipped for battle?

Scorpions are protected with tough leathery armor. They also have many weapons – jagged jaws, huge pincers and a poisonous sting in their tail. Some have stings as venomous as a cobra's bite.

Is it true?

Ants can fire acid at their enemies.

YES. Wood ants fire a stinging acid from their abdomens. Ants can be dangerous little creatures. They can bite, and then squirt acid into the wound.

What spits at its prey?

All spiders produce silk, but only about half use silk to make webs or traps to catch prey. Other spiders hunt or pounce on their victims. The spitting spider lives up to its name. It catches prey by shooting sticky poisonous gum at it, fired through its fangs.

Spitting spider

57

? What uses a trapdoor to catch its prey?

The trapdoor spider builds an underground burrow, lined with silk and covered with a hinged lid. It lifts up the lid just a little, peeps out and waits. When prey approaches, it flips open the trapdoor, leaps out and attacks.

Trapdoor spider

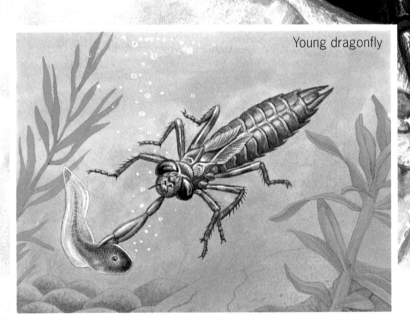

Young dragonfly

? What catches its victims with its lip?

Young dragonflies live in ponds and streams. They catch tadpoles and small fish using a special lower lip, which shoots out to stab and hold prey.

Is it true?
Wasps will not attack spiders.

NO. The sting of the large spider wasp can paralyze a spider three times its size. The wasp then lays an egg on the spider. When the larva hatches it eats the spider alive.

Amazing! Spider webs come in many shapes and sizes. The purse web spider spins a long, tube-shaped web. The spider waits inside the web until an unsuspecting insect lands on the outside of the web. Then it bites through the silk and catches its prey.

Millipede

Jumping spider

What creeps up on its prey?

The jumping spider stalks its prey like a cat, before suddenly pouncing. Even with eight eyes, most spiders are short-sighted, and rely on hairs on their legs to sense vibrations. But jumping spiders have excellent eyesight.

When is an ant not an ant?

When it's a 'jar'. Honeypot ants store nectar and honeydew when there are lots of flowers in bloom. They use some of the workers as 'jars'. They fill them with nectar until they are so fat they cannot move. The ants are 'milked' later when flowers are not so plentiful.

Honeypot ant

Is it true?
All mosquitoes suck blood.

NO. Only female mosquitoes suck blood. They can't lay their eggs without it. In the hotter parts of the world, biting insects can pass on diseases to humans. Malaria is carried by mosquitoes. It kills over one million people each year.

Mosquito

Amazing! There are insects that eat wool, leather, tobacco, books, blood, carpets – just about anything in the world you can think of. One insect, the male minotaur beetle, presents rabbit droppings to its mate as a tasty treat for her eggs!

What makes a bug a bug?

Bugs are a group of insects which all have a hollow needle-like tube that grows from their mouths. They use this 'beak' to suck up juices. Some live on the sap of plants. Others suck fluids from other insects and small animals.

Assassin bug feeding on a caterpillar

Which insect drinks with a straw?

Nearly all butterflies have a long hollow tongue called a proboscis which they use to suck up nectar. They keep their tongues curled up under their heads when they are not drinking.

61

? Which insect lights up the sky when it's courting?

Male fireflies have special chemicals inside their bodies to make flashing light displays while searching for a mate. The females can't fly, but also send out light signals to help the males find them.

Dancing spiders

Is it true?
Spiders dance to show off.

YES. Male spiders perform courtship dances in front of female spiders. When they find a mate, male spiders have to be careful. The female may be much larger. The dance helps the male persuade the female to mate with him, instead of eat him.

Firefly

Why do crickets sing?

Male crickets and grasshoppers 'sing' to attract a mate. They rub their front wings together to make the noise, which is louder in hot weather.

Amazing!

Queen ants have wings at first. But after they've flown off and found a mate, they pull or rub their wings off. They no longer need them, because they are going to spend the rest of their lives producing eggs.

Praying mantis

Whose mate meets a horrid end?

The mantis eats its prey alive. For the female praying mantis, that includes her mate. She begins to eat the male while they are still mating.

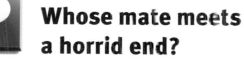

Who makes a good mom?

A female earwig looks after its eggs and young for several months. It keeps the eggs clean and warm, and feeds the young with food from its own stomach.

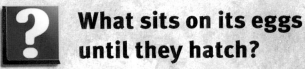

What sits on its eggs until they hatch?

Some shield bugs protect their eggs by sitting on them. This keeps them safe from hungry predators. After hatching, they look after their young until they can move about.

Shield bug

Amazing! Many bees and wasps live alone. The potter wasp makes a small vase-shaped nest out of clay and saliva. It lays just one egg in it. It then stocks the nest with food for the larva, seals it up and flies off to make another vase.

Potter wasp

? How do baby scorpions travel?

Unlike spiders, insects and other creepy-crawlies, scorpions give birth to live young. Some of them are cared for by the mother who carries the whole brood on her back. If one of the young falls off, she places her pincers on the ground so that it can climb back up again.

Scorpion and young

Is it true?
A queen bee lays up to 3,500 eggs a day.

YES. Most creepy-crawlies produce large numbers of eggs. This makes sure that at least some survive to adulthood without getting eaten.

What lives in a skyscraper?

Termites build air-conditioned mounds that can be 20 feet tall. These nests contain a maze of tunnels and can be home to millions of termites. Each colony has a king, a queen and soldiers to guard it. In countries with a very wet climate, some termites build mounds with umbrella-shaped tops.

Termite mound

Is it true?
An ant's nest is full of different rooms.

YES. The nest is made up of many separate chambers, connected by a maze of tunnels. Some rooms are nurseries for the eggs and young, others are food cupboards and some are trash cans.

Queen termite

What makes a nest in a tree?

Weaver ants make nests by pulling leaves together on a branch. They stick the leaf edges together using sticky silk which they gently squeeze from the ant larvae.

Weaver ants

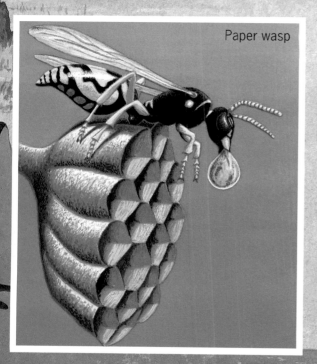

Paper wasp

What makes a paper nest?

Paper wasps build nests out of thin sheets of paper. They make the paper themselves by scraping wood from dead trees with their jaws and mixing it with saliva.

Amazing! Like ants and termites, honeybees live with thousands of others in colonies. They work together to find food, care for the young and protect the nest. The nest is made from waxy material which they shape into honeycomb. Honeybee nests are very strong and can last for 50 years.

What helps around the house?

The spiders you see scurrying around your home can be very useful to us. They help get rid of pests, such as flies which carry germs, and there are helpful creepy-crawlies in the garden, too. Hoverflies and ladybugs eat greenfly, and earthworms help improve the soil.

House spider

Dust mite seen through a powerful microscope

Amazing! Most homes are full of creepy-crawlies, often too small to see without a magnifying glass. Moth larvae eat wool, booklice feed on books, carpet beetles munch carpets, silver fish scuttle under baths, furniture beetles tunnel through furniture, fleas live on cats and dogs, cockroaches lurk behind cookers.

Flea

Who has been sleeping in my bed?

Dust mites are smaller than a period. They live all over the house, but they particularly like beds. Bedbugs are now quite rare, but in some countries they feed on sleeping people.

Is it true?

Spiders get into the bath tub by climbing up the drainpipe and through the drain.

NO. It's more likely that they fall down the tub's slippery sides, while roaming around our houses looking for a mate.

Who has been in the cookie jar?

Many creepy-crawlies like to live around food. Cheese mites lay their eggs on cheese. Spider beetles eat spices and sauce mixes. An old bag of flour may contain mites, caterpillars and beetles. Guess what the biscuit beetle prefers? Hard dry ones luckily, not stickie cookies.

CHAPTER THREE

SNAKES

AND OTHER REPTILES

Snake

? What are reptiles?

Reptiles are a group of animals that includes snakes, lizards, turtles, tortoises, alligators and crocodiles. They are all vertebrates (they have bones and skeletons inside their bodies), they breathe air and most of them live on land. Their skins are scaly to stop their bodies drying out.

Lizard

 Amazing! Lizards love sunbathing. All reptiles are cold-blooded. They can't control their own body temperature but rely on the weather instead. Cold lizards are sluggish and slow. So they warm up in the sun, then scurry off hunting.

Turtle

Which is the shortest snake?

At only about four inches long, thread snakes are the shortest, thinnest snakes in the world. If you took the lead out of a pencil, they could slither through the hole. These rare snakes live in the West Indies, and eat tiny ants and termites.

Thread Snake

Is it true?

Today's reptiles have famous relatives.

YES. The relatives of today's reptiles were the dinosaurs, which ruled the Earth for more than 200 million years. They suddenly died out about 65 million years ago.

Which is the biggest reptile?

The biggest reptiles alive today are saltwater crocodiles. They're usually about 13 feet long, but a gigantic crocodile killed in 1957 measured no less than 28 feet, and weighed more than two tons.

Saltwater crocodile

? Why do snakes shed their skin?

As a snake grows, its scaly skin gets too small. So the snake grows a new skin underneath, then slithers out of the old one, starting from the head and working down to the tail. A snake sheds its skin in one piece, several times a year.

Is it true?
You can tell a tortoise's age from its shell.

YES. A tortoise's shell is made of bone, covered in tough, horny plates. The shell protects the tortoise's body. But that's not all it's good for. Each year, the plates grow a new ring. Count these up, and you can use them to estimate the tortoise's age.

Which reptile has armor plating?

Alligators and crocodiles are covered in tough, horny scales, strengthened with bone. This waterproof armor stops their bodies drying out in the sun, and protects them from enemies.

Reticulated python

 Amazing! Geckos have see-through eyelids. These are clear flaps of skin which protect their eyes from dust and dirt. A gecko can't blink to clean its eyelids. So it sticks out its tongue and licks them clean.

Which snake uses a rattle?

The rattle at the tip of a rattlesnake's tail is made of hollow scales, loosely linked together. If an enemy gets too close, the rattlesnake shakes its rattle, which makes a loud, angry buzzing sound to scare the attacker away. If this doesn't work, the rattlesnake coils itself up, then strikes with its poisonous fangs.

Which is the most poisonous land snake?

Some of the deadliest land snakes live in Australia. A drop of their poison could kill 250,000 mice. Other highly dangerous snakes include cobras, rattlesnakes, and taipans, which can grow to eleven feet long.

Which snake spits poison?

One type of cobra spits poison in its enemies' faces, blinding the victim! Spitting cobras have very good aims. They can hit a target more than six feet away.

Spitting cobra

Amazing! Fer-de-lance snakes have massive fangs and are deadly poisonous. They prey on rats and mice. Explorers claimed that local hunters in South America put these lethal snakes in tubes and fired them at their enemies.

Is it true?
All lizards are poisonous.

NO. Of the 3,800 different kinds of lizards, only two are poisonous. They are the gila monster and the Mexican beaded lizard. These lizards do not have fangs but bite their vicitims and chew poison into the wound instead.

Gila monster

Beaded lizard

Inland taipan

Which snake has the longest fangs?
The deadly gaboon viper from Africa has fangs which grow up to two inches, as long as your pinkie! When they're not in use, they're folded back against the roof of the viper's mouth.

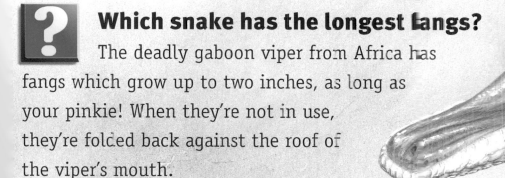

Gaboon viper

What was the largest snake snack ever eaten?

The largest snack ever eaten by a snake was an impala antelope. It was devoured by an African rock python. The snake didn't chew its enormous meal into pieces. It swallowed the impala whole!

Rock python

Impala

Which snake squeezes its prey to death?

A boa constrictor holds its prey in its teeth, then wraps its coils tightly around it. The snake does not crush its victim to death but squeezes it until it suffocates.

Is it true?

A snake can go for more than three years without food.

YES. It can take a snake weeks to digest a large meal. So they don't need to eat very often. A pit viper once survived without food for three years, three months - a world record.

Why do snakes have elastic jaws?

A snake has sharp, backward-pointing teeth. Its teeth are good at holding food but can't bite it into chunks. Instead, snakes swallow their prey whole. Snakes have amazingly stretchy jaws, with elastic-like hinges between their jawbones. This means they can open their mouths very wide, to swallow food larger than the size of their heads, such as eggs.

Amazing! There are many scary stories of snakes swallowing people. But only a few of them are true. In 1979, a young boy in South Africa was seized by a 14 feet-long African rock python. His friends ran off to get help. When they came back about 20 minutes later, the snake had swallowed the boy whole.

NO. Crocodiles do find people tasty, especially if they're hungry. It's estimated that saltwater crocodiles kill and eat up to 2,000 people each year.

Which lizard uses its tongue as a catapult?

A chameleon has a very long, sticky tongue. When it spots a tasty insect, it shoots out its tongue like a catapult, catches the insect and pulls it in. All in a split second.

Chameleon

Amazing! Alligators and crocodiles can snap their ferocious jaws shut with terrible force, but the muscles for opening their mouths up again are surprisingly weak. All you need to keep a crocodile's mouth shut is an elastic band. But keep your fingers away from those sharp, pointed teeth!

80

❓ Which lizard stores food in its tail?

The gila monster lives in the desert It feeds on insects, birds' eggs and rodents. When there's plenty of food, it eats more than it needs and stores some as fat in its tail. It lives off this store when food is short.

Gila monster

Marine iguana

❓ Which lizard loves seaweed?

The marine iguana lives on the Galapagos Islands. It loves eating seaweed. At low tide, it dives into the water and clings on to a weed-covered rock with its claws. It tears off the seaweed with its mouth.

❓ Which snake pretends to be poisonous?

The milk snake lives in the rainforests of Central America. It's shy, secretive and harmless, but its bright bands of red, yellow and black make it look like the deadly coral snake. Its enemies think the milk snake is equally poisonous, and so leave it well alone.

Coral snake

Milk snake

Is it true?
Some snakes mimic vines.

YES. The African vine snake hangs down from tree branches, looking just like a harmless vine. There's a nasty suprise for any bird that perches on it. It suddenly snatches the bird and swallows it down.

Vine snake

Which snake looks like sand?

Many desert snakes are perfectly camouflaged to look like sand. The horned viper lies in the sand with just its 'horns' showing. When a tasty desert rat passes by, the snake pounces.

 Amazing! Chameleons are brilliant at changing color. They can go from almost white to black in minutes. They change color to blend in with their surroundings and to show they are feeling angry or frightened.

Where do leaf-tailed geckos hide?

Pressed upside down against a tree trunk, the leaf-tailed gecko is almost impossible to see. Its body and tail are dappled brown and green to look exactly like the bark of the tree. The ragged fringe of scales around its body and legs hides its outline. It lives on the island of Madagascar.

Leaf-tailed gecko

Who walks upside down?

Geckos can run up smooth walls and walk upside down across ceilings. They have special suction pads on their feet which allow them to cling on. The pads are covered in thousands of tiny hairs which help the geckos to grip the tiniest bumps and dips.

Gecko

Basilisk lizard

 ## Which lizard walks on water?

The basilisk lizard escapes from enemies by running across the water. It runs so fast on its long, fringed back toes that it doesn't have time to sink. The lizard lives by rivers in South American forests.

Amazing! Tortoises are real slow pokes. Their heavy shells weigh them down so much that they move about very slowly, or not at all. Most tortoises lumber along at speeds of less than 0.3 mph, even when they're hungry.

Which lizard runs the fastest?

The speediest lizard is the spiny-tailed iguana. It can speed along at almost 22 mph, about the same speed as a champion sprinter. In an experiment, a racetrack was set up and the lizards were timed with the same devices used at the Olympic Games.

Is it true?
Dragons can fly.

YES. Flying dragons are small lizards. To travel through the trees, they take to the air. They glide from branch to branch on special 'wings'. These are flaps of skin stretched over very long ribs which stick out from the sides of their body.

Flying dragon

Which snake can fly?

The paradise flying snake can glide for 100 feet or more between the trees. It launches itself from a branch, using its tail to steer. Its body acts like a parachute, trapping air underneath, slowing it down as it floats down and lands on a lower branch.

Amazing! The fastest land snake is the deadly black mamba. There are tales of them overtaking galloping horses. This isn't true but these speedy snakes can race along at about 12 mph.

Black mamba

Can snakes climb trees?

Many snakes slither through the trees, after birds and insects to eat. They are excellent climbers, with rough scales on the underside of their bodies to help them grip slippery branches.

How do snakes slither across loose sand?

Sidewinders have an unusual way of slithering across loose, shifting sand. The sand makes it difficult to get a firm grip. So they flip their bodies sideways in a series of large loops. It leaves a tell-tale set of lines behind in the sand, like the tracks of a bulldozer.

Flying snake

Is it true?
Snakes once had legs.

YES. The ancestors of snakes were lizard-like creatures with two pairs of legs. Snakes today do not have legs. Their skeletons are made of a skull, a long backbone and many pairs of ribs. This gives snakes a long, thin shape for slithering across the ground.

Do all reptiles lay eggs?

Most reptiles lay eggs with tough shells to protect the babies inside. But some types of snakes and lizards give birth to live young. When they are born, they look like miniature versions of their parents.

Which reptile eats its babies?

Large alligators only eat smaller ones during food shortages, and sometimes that includes their own young! When alligator babies hatch, their mother picks them up in her mouth and carries them safely to the water.

Alligator and young

Amazing! Most snakes don't look after their eggs at all. But pythons are caring parents. The females coil their bodies around their eggs to guard them from attack. They also shiver and shake their coils slightly to keep the eggs warm.

Green tree python

Green turtle

 Which babies are born on a beach?

Sea turtles come ashore to lay their eggs in nests on the beach. The female covers them with sand, then goes back to the sea. The eggs take about a month to hatch.

 Is it true?
Baby green tree pythons are green.

NO. Baby green tree pythons are yellow or red. They don't change color to green until they're two years old.

89

Is it true?

Some geckos bark like dogs.

YES. The barking gecko and the tokay gecko both bark like dogs. They use their loud voices to attract mates or defend their territory.

Spectacled cobra

How well can snakes hear?

Snakes can't hear at all. They have no outer ears for detecting sounds. Instead, they pick up vibrations in the ground through their bodies. Snake charmers make it look as if a snake is dancing to the sound of music. But the snake is actually following the movement of the snake charmer's pipe with its eyes, ready to attack.

 Amazing! Crocodiles and alligators are very noisy. They cough, hiss and bellow to attract mates and keep in touch with their group. The American alligator roars like a lion. It can be heard about 500 feet away.

How do snakes smell with their tongues?

Snakes don't smell things through their noses like we do. They pick up smell with their tongues, which they flick in and out. They can recognize different smells with the Jacobson's organ in the roof of the mouth.

Jacobson's organ

Which reptile can look in two ways at once?

Chameleons can move each of their large, bulging eyes on its own. This means they can look in two ways at once. When they're hunting, one eye can look out for tasty insects to eat. The other can watch out for hungry enemies.

Chameleon

Why do skinks stick out their tongues?

When a blue-tongued skink is threatened, it simply sticks out its bright blue tongue. Its enemies quickly run away. Skinks are types of lizards. The biggest skinks grow to over two feet, as long as your arm.

Blue-tongued skink

Hognosed snake

Frilled lizard

Is it true?

Hognosed snakes imitate rattlesnakes.

YES. A hognosed snake has an ingenious way of protecting itself from enemies. It pretends to be a deadly poisonous rattlesnake. It rubs its tail against its body to make a sinister rattling sound. If this fails, the snake rolls on to its back and pretends to be dead.

Which turtle smells terrible?

The tiny stinkpot turtle lives in North America. It spends most of its time in slow-moving streams. As well as its shell, the turtle has a secret weapon to use against its enemies. It gives off a truly terrible smell!

92

How do frilled lizards scare off attackers?

If a frilled lizard is chased into a corner, it puts on a dramatic show. It faces its attacker, with mouth wide open, and fans out the huge frill of skin around its neck. Then it sways from side to side, while hissing menacingly. It might look frightening, but in fact it's a fairly harmless lizard.

Amazing!

If its tail is grabbed by an enemy, a lizard simply runs off and leaves its tail behind. The tail breaks off at a special weak spot between the tail bones. Luckily, the lizard can grow a brand-new tail, although it is often shorter than the old one.

Amazing! Water skinks have anti-freeze in their blood. Special chemicals stop their blood freezing even if the temperature falls below zero. This means that the skinks can come out of hibernation when there is still snow on the ground. Water skinks live in the mountains of eastern Australia.

Black rattlesnake

? How does a horned lizard warn off enemies?

The horned lizard is an odd-looking reptile, covered in prickly spines. If it's attacked, it has a weird way of defending itself. It sprays blood from its eyes. This may fool its enemy into thinking it's wounded and leaving it alone.

Horned lizard

Which turtle uses its neck as a snorkel?

The matamata turtle lives in slow-moving rivers in South America. It lurks on the riverbed, with its mouth wide open, waiting to snap up passing prey. It uses its long neck as a snorkel to hold its nostrils out of the water. In this way, it can breathe without having to swim up to the surface.

Matamata turtle

Is it true?
Crocodiles cry real tears.

YES. Saltwater crocodiles look as if they are crying. But it's not because they are sad. They cry to get rid of extra salt which they take in with their food. People use the saying 'crocodile tears' to mean pretend tears.

Armadillo lizard

Which lizard looks like an armadillo?

The armadillo lizard has tough, armor-like skin on its head and back, just like a real armadillo. To escape from enemies, it hides in a crack in the rock, or it curls up into a tight, scaly ball to protect its soft stomach.

Amazing! The lizard-like tuatara is the only survivor of a group of reptiles that lived in the time of the dinosaurs. By 65 million years ago, the rest of the group had died out. Only the tuatara was left. Tuataras are only found in New Zealand. Their name means 'spiny backed' in the local Maori language.

Reticulated python

? Which is the longest snake?

The giant reticulated python can measure up to 33 feet long. That's longer than six bicycles standing end to end. No snake could grow longer than 50 feet. It would be too heavy to move.

Komodo dragon

Is it true?

Sea snakes are the most poisonous snakes.

YES. All sea snakes are poisonous. One of the most poisonous of all is the banded sea snake from around Australia. Its venom is many times stronger than the deadliest land snake. Luckily, this snake rarely bites human beings.

Sea snake

 ## Which is the biggest lizard?

The Komodo dragon is the world's largest lizard. Males can grow to more than nine feet long and weigh more than 330 pounds. These record-breaking reptiles live on a few islands in Indonesia. They are meat-eaters and can swallow deer and pigs whole!

Which reptile lives the longest?

Tortoises live longer than any other animals on land. The oldest tortoise known was a Marion's tortoise from the Seychelles. When it died in 1918, it was thought to be over 150 years old.

? Which is the smallest lizard?

A little gecko from the Caribbean is the world's smallest lizard. This tiny reptile is only just over an inch long. That's about as long as your thumb.

British Virgin Island gecko

? Which is the largest turtle?

The leatherback turtle is about the size of a small car. This giant reptile can grow almost ten feet long, from its head to the tip of its tail. It measures nearly ten feet across its front flippers. It can weigh almost a ton.

Leatherback turtle

Is it true?

Most poisonous snakes live in Africa.

NO. Eight out of ten of the world's deadliest snakes live in Australia. About 3,000 people are bitten by snakes there every year. Luckily, very few of these snakebites are fatal.

Dwarf caiman

Which is the smallest crocodile?

The smallest crocodile is the dwarf caiman which lives in South America. This mini crocodile only grows about five feet long, about a third of the size of its giant cousin, the massive saltwater crocodile.

Amazing! At almost a quarter of a ton, the anaconda from South America is the world's bulkiest snake. This heavyweight snake lies in slow-moving rivers or streams, waiting for prey to come down to drink. Then it grabs its victim in its mouth and squeezes it to death.

CHAPTER FOUR

SHARKS

AND OTHER DANGEROUS FISH

❓ What are sharks?

Sharks are meat-eating sea fish. Most have sleek bodies and rows of sharp teeth. There are about 375 types, of different shapes and sizes, living in different parts of the world. The dwarf shark is only four inches long, while the whale shark, the biggest of all fish, is 50 feet.

Hammerhead shark

 Amazing!

Sharks become sluggish in cool water, and so most prefer to live in warm seas. But the huge Greenland shark, 20 feet long, enjoys icy water. It lives in the North Atlantic, hunting for fish and seals beneath the pack ice.

Megalodon tooth

❓ How old are sharks?

Fossils show that sharks appeared more than 350 million years ago, long before the dinosaurs. Megalodon was a huge shark which hunted large prey and probably ate shellfish too. Its teeth were about three inches long.

Whale shark

Manta ray

Basking shark

Is it true?
All sharks are dangerous.

NO. In the order of dangerous sharks, the great white is most feared by people. But most sharks are harmless to us, and will only attack if they are disturbed. Other dangerous sharks include the tiger shark, mako, bronze and black-tipped whalers, and hammerhead.

Are sharks different from other fish?

Sharks, and their relatives the skates and rays, have skeletons made of rubbery cartilage. Other fish have skeletons made of bone. A shark's gill slits are not covered like other fish, but are in a row behind its head.

103

How fast can a shark swim?

Sharks such as the mako shark are perfect swimming machines, capable of speeds of up to 45 mph. Their sleek shape means they can move quickly through the water and turn at speed.

Is it true?
Sharks never have a break.

NO. Sharks living near the surface must swim all their lives to avoid sinking. But others like the nurse shark spend most of their time motionless on the seabed. Nurse sharks can pump water over their gills and so they don't need to keep moving.

Gray reef shark

Why are sharks darker on top?

Sharks which swim near the surface are dark on top and paler on their undersides. This means they are difficult to see from above or below as they hunt for prey.

Blue shark

 Amazing! Most sharks drown if they stop swimming, as no oxygen-rich water is passing over their gills. They also sink. They do not have a swim bladder like other fish. They have a huge oily liver instead, which helps to keep them afloat.

? **How do sharks breathe?**
Like all fish, sharks extract oxygen from the water using their gills. Water enters their mouths, and oxygen is absorbed as the water passes over the red, feathery, blood-filled gills. Most sharks keep moving all the time in order to get a constant supply of oxygen.

Water leaves through gill slits

Oxygen-rich water enters mouth

105

Sand tiger shark

Do sharks have the same senses as us?

Sharks have the five senses of sight, smell, taste, hearing and touch. They also have one more. Sensitive cells on their snouts allow them to pick up tiny electrical signals from other animals.

Reef sharks

How do sharks know when an animal is struggling nearby?

Sharks can tell that there are animals in their area, even when there is no blood to smell. A sensitive 'lateral line' along their bodies allows them to feel ripples in the water from any struggling animal or person.

Lateral line

Do sharks have good eyesight?

Sight is important in the final moments of a shark's hunt. But sharks depend much more on their sense of smell. Sharks get very excited at the smell of blood. They can smell a drop of blood, diluted millions of times, nearly half a mile away.

Amazing! Most fish have scaly skin, but a shark's tough skin and scales are very different. They are sharp points called denticles which are like teeth. Shark skin was once used for smoothing down wood, instead of sandpaper.

Is it true?
Sharks nudge their food before they take a bite.

YES. They sometimes nudge an object or animal with their snout before they decide whether to eat it or not! Perhaps they can 'taste' it with special cells in their skin.

Denticles

107

What eats its unborn brothers and sisters?

Some sharks give birth to only a few baby sharks, or pups. This is because the first pups to develop eat the other eggs and embryos inside the mother. Often only one mako pup survives because it eats all the others.

Adult and young mako

Amazing! Some sharks take nine months to develop inside the mother, as long as a human baby. But the spiny dogfish takes 24 months! Young sharks are then on their own, even though it may be years before they are ready for the open sea.

Do sharks lay eggs?

In most sharks, fertilized eggs develop inside the female's body. But some sharks lay eggs and then swim away, leaving the eggs to develop on their own. Dogfish lay eggs in leathery cases, which are called 'mermaid's purses'.

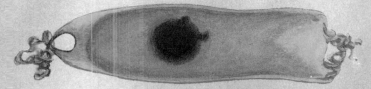
Swell shark embryo at one-month-old

Three-month-old embryo

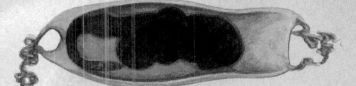
Seven-month-old embryo

Is it true?
Sharks never eat their own young.

NO. Some sharks give birth, and then if they come across their pup later in the day they will eat it!

Hammerhead shark pups

What gives birth to lots of pups?

As many as 40 hammerhead shark pups may be born in one litter. They develop in a similar way to human babies, inside their mother's body.

What is known as the trash can of the sea?

Tiger sharks will eat anything. They are not put off by a crunchy turtle shell, or a stinging jellyfish, or even a poisonous snake. They will happily munch dead animals that have been washed out to sea, old boots, papers, tin cans, plastic bags – and even people!

Amazing! Sometimes when a shark feeds, others join in. They get excited at the blood and movement around them, and seem to go crazy, biting, twisting and turning wildly in a 'feeding frenzy'.

Tiger shark

How many teeth do sharks have?

Sharks are born with jaws full of teeth, neatly arranged in rows. They grow teeth all their lives. When front ones wear out or are lost, they're replaced by new teeth behind.

Sand tiger shark

Is it true?
A shark's teeth last for months.

NO. Once a rear tooth has moved to the front row, it may drop out, snap off or be worn away in as little as two weeks.

Do all sharks have the same teeth?

The shape and size depend on a shark's food. For example, the great white has slicing teeth for tearing off chunks of seal or dolphin. The Port Jackson has sharp front teeth to hold shellfish, and blunt back teeth to crush them.

Tiger shark tooth

Mako tooth

Great white shark tooth

Amazing! It's almost impossible for sharks to get rid of parasites. Tiny creatures eat parasite eggs, fish eat the tiny creatures, and then sharks eat the fish!

Is it true?
Remora fish will feed inside a shark's mouth.

YES. A whale shark is so big that there's lots of space for remoras. Some attach themselves to the whale shark's mouth and will even swim inside the mouth and gills to find food.

Lemon shark with remoras

Pilot fish

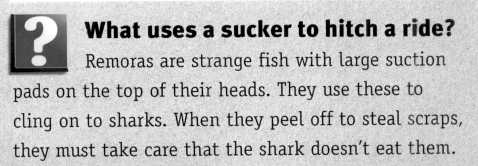

What uses a sucker to hitch a ride?
Remoras are strange fish with large suction pads on the top of their heads. They use these to cling on to sharks. When they peel off to steal scraps, they must take care that the shark doesn't eat them.

Which travelers harm sharks?

Tiny creatures called parasites feed on a shark's skin, inside its guts and in its blood. Some even settle and feed on the surface of its eye, making it difficult for the shark to see.

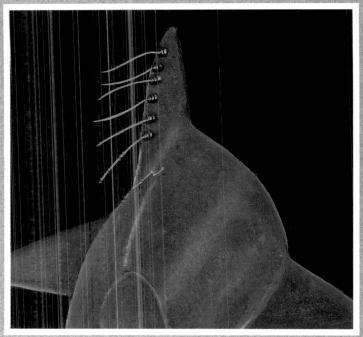

Parasites feeding on a shark's fin

What hides in a shark's shadow?

Just like remoras, pilot fish also travel with sharks. They're quick and agile as they swim alongside the shark. They hide in the shark's shadow, safe from their enemies, and dart out to snap up any left-overs from the latest kill.

113

❓ What can attack with its tail?

The thresher shark has a long and powerful tail, often longer than its main body, which it uses like a whip. Like dolphins, thresher sharks hunt in packs. They use their tails to stun fish or to round them up ready for attack.

Thresher sharks

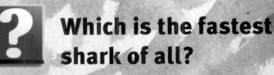

Seal

Mako shark

❓ Which is the fastest shark of all?

The mako shark can move through water as quickly as 45 mph. If an angler catches one, it sometimes leaps out of the water into the air as it tries to escape.

What can swallow a seal whole?

The great white shark, also known as 'white death', is a powerful predator that often swallows its prey whole. Luckily, it thinks that seals and sea lions are much tastier than human beings!

Amazing! Bull sharks are unusual because they prefer shark meat to other flesh. They're one of few sharks to spend time in fresh water. They swim up rivers and can enter lakes.

Great white shark

Is it true?
Sharks have to eat every day.

NO. After a good kill, a great white shark could last three months without food before it needs to eat again.

? Which is the biggest fish in the world?

The biggest fish is also one of the most harmless, the whale shark. It measures 50 feet long and weighs about 13 tons. It swims slowly through the sea with its mouth open wide, filtering millions of tiny creatures from the water.

Is it true?

You could hitch a ride on a whale shark.

YES. These gentle giants have been known to allow scuba divers to hang on to their fins and ride with them.

Whale shark

Amazing! Little is known about the megamouth. But we do know that it has luminous organs that give off a glow around its lips. Scientists think this may be to tempt tiny creatures into its mouth.

Basking shark

? Which shark appears to sunbathe?

Basking sharks spend much of their time wallowing at the ocean's surface, especially when it's sunny – probably because there's more food there on sunny days, not because they want a suntan!

Megamouth

? What has a huge mouth?

The megamouth shark lives in deep, dark seas. Like the whale shark, it swims with its enormous mouth wide open, filtering water for food. It is very rare and only a few have ever been seen.

117

Which shark has wings?

Angel sharks have very large pectoral fins, like an angel's wings. They spend much of their lives on the ocean floor, waiting for fish or shellfish to come along so they can snap them up.

Is it true?

Angel sharks look like monks.

YES. Angel sharks are also called monkfish because their heads are the same shape as a monk's hood.

Angel shark

Port Jackson shark

What is a 'pig fish'?

The Port Jackson shark is known as the 'pig fish', or 'bulldog shark'. It has a blunt head and a squashed nose with very large nostrils for finding sea urchins and shellfish.

Which shark uses a disguise?

The wobbegong shark is a master of disguise. The coloring and markings of its flattened body help it blend into its surroundings on the seabed. It also has a 'beard' of skin around its mouth which looks just like seaweed to unsuspecting prey.

Amazing!
If a swell shark is attacked by a predator, it gulps down as much sea water as it can, and swells up like a balloon. It then jams itself into a crack in a rock where its enemy can't reach it.

Wobbegong

Which mysterious shark has a very long snout?

Goblin sharks were discovered 100 years ago and yet we still know very little about them. They live in deep water, and use their long, sensitive snouts to seek out prey.

Goblin shark

What has a head like a hammer?

The head of a hammerhead shark is spread out to form a T-shape with its body. Its eyes are on each end of the 'hammer'. As it swims, it swings its head from side to side so it can look around.

Hammerhead shark

Is it true?

Cookiecutter sharks can glow.

YES. These small sharks have light organs on their undersides, which glow, maybe to persuade their prey to come close to them.

Seal wounded by cookiecutter

Cookiecutter

? What bites chunks out of its prey?

Cookiecutter sharks are often happy with just a bite or two from their prey, which includes whales, seals and dolphins. The wounds they make with their small teeth are oval-shaped, a bit like a cookie.

Amazing!

Hammerhead sharks have few enemies and they feed alone. Yet they sometimes gather together in large 'schools', where hundreds all swim together.

YES. Sawfish and saw sharks have long sharp snouts studded with teeth, like a saw. They use their snouts to dig in the mud for food and to slash at other fish. The six types of sawfish belong to the same group as rays.

Manta ray

❓ What is called the devilfish?

Manta rays are also known as devilfish, even though they are harmless and feed on plankton. They are the largest of all rays, at 23 feet across. They flap their huge fins like wings, which makes them look as if they're flying slowly and gracefully through the water.

Electric ray

Amazing! Rays and skates may look very different from sharks, but they are closely related. They all have gill slits instead of gill covers and skeletons made of rubbery cartilage.

Which fish can shock?

The electric ray has special electric organs just behind its head. It gives off bursts of electricity to defend itself or to stun the fish it feeds on.

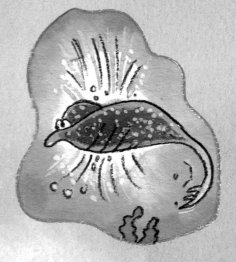

What has a sting on its tail?

Stingrays have poisonous spines on their whip-like tails. Some have one poisonous spine, others have several. They lie on the seabed with only their eyes and tail showing.

Stingray

Is it true?
Barracudas are attracted to jewelery.

YES. In waters where barracudas are found, swimmers should take off any jewelery in case a passing barracuda takes a fancy to it!

Which eel becomes a fierce hunter?

When moray eels are young, they eat shrimps and tiny fish. But as they grow up, they learn to prey on larger and larger creatures.

Moray eel

Which tiny fish can strip an animal bare in minutes?

Piranhas live in rivers in South America where they hunt together in shoals of hundreds. With powerful jaws full of razor-sharp teeth, they may attack any large animal that enters the water.

Stonefish

When is a stone not a stone?

When it's a stonefish. Stonefish are camouflaged so that it's almost impossible to see them amongst the rocks on the seabed. But sharp poisonous spines on their backs make them very dangerous to step on.

Piranha fish

Amazing! Many fish living in the cold, dark depths of the ocean look like monsters. They may have huge mouths full of sharp teeth, most are black and many can produce their own light.

125

Shark-proof bag

Amazing! In Australia in the 1930s, hundreds of sharks were caught in nets in just a few months. The numbers of many large sharks have gone down sharply all over the world because of hunting.

? How can we prevent shark attacks?

Sharks have often attacked people who have survived shipwrecks or plane crashes far out at sea. Inflatable bags have been tested, which sharks tend to avoid. They can't detect moving limbs, electrical signals or blood inside them. Beaches can be protected by nets.

Great white shark

Is it true?
Nothing attacks a shark.

NO. Sharks will attack each other. They are also attacked by whales, and even dolphins who will group together to protect their young. But the biggest threat of all comes from people.

Why do sharks attack?

When a shark attacks, it is often because it mistakes a swimmer or surfer for a seal or other prey. About 100 shark attacks are recorded on people each year. Many of the victims survive.

Surfer on board

Seal

Shark cage

Who swims inside a cage?

Scientists studying dangerous sharks, such as the ocean white-tip and bull shark, often protect themselves inside a cage. The shark can bang the cage as much as it likes, but the diver is safe inside.

❓ How can we learn more about sharks?

These days, people are more keen to learn about sharks. You can visit an aquarium to watch and find out more about these fascinating fish.

Amazing! Scientists can now tell a lot from some sharks' behavior. By studying a creature's movements and senses, they know when a shark is just being nosy, or when it's about to attack. By learning more, we may kill fewer sharks, and suffer fewer shark attacks.

❓ Why do people kill sharks?

People kill millions of sharks every year, some to protect swimmers, others for food or just for sport. If too many are killed, sharks might disappear altogether.

Fisherman and catch

Which scientists dress like knights of old?

Scientists studying sharks sometimes wear chain-mail suits for protection. They may tag a shark's fins to learn how quickly and far it can travel.

Diver in chain-mail with blue shark

Is it true?
We've discovered all the sharks that exist.

NO. Megamouth was first seen in 1976. Scientists think that there might be more sharks waiting to be discovered in the depths of the oceans.

CHAPTER FIVE

BIRDS OF PREY

AND OTHER FEATHERED FRIENDS

Which are the biggest birds?

The African ostrich can grow to over eight feet tall, which is much taller than the average man. The huge wandering albatross has the largest wingspan in the world, at nearly ten feet. Its long, pointed wings make it an excellent glider.

Ostrich

Amazing! There are around 9,000 different kinds of birds, in many colors, shapes and sizes. They live all over world, in steamy jungles, icy regions, by the sea, in towns, and some move from one area to another when they migrate.

Which are the smallest birds?

Hummingbirds are the smallest birds in world. The bee hummingbird of Cuba is no bigger than a bumblebee! Hummingbirds can flap their wings at up to 90 beats per second. They get their name from the humming sound their wings make.

Rufous hummingbird

Albatross

What are birds?

Birds all have two legs, two wings, a beak, they lay eggs and they are the only animals that have feathers. But not all birds can fly, and not all flying animals are birds.

Is it true?
The first bird dates back to dinosaur times.

Black-faced ant thrush

YES. Archaeopteryx is the earliest bird-like creature that we know of. It lived 150 million years ago. It had a head like a reptile, sharp teeth, a long tail and feathered wings.

133

Sparrowhawk

❓ What is a bird of prey?

Birds of prey catch and eat other animals. They are excellent hunters, with strong hooked beaks and sharp claws called talons, which they use to kill and tear at prey.

❓ Why are birds of prey good hunters?

The eyes of a bird of prey are different from other birds' eyes. They're very big, and face forwards so they can judge detail and distance well. A buzzard's eyes are as big as yours!

Buzzard

Amazing! Eagles can catch animals much bigger and heavier than themselves. The harpy eagle, which lives in South American jungles, is the biggest eagle of all. It has huge feet which it uses for grabbing and crushing monkeys and other animals.

134

Is it true?

Some birds eat eggs.

YES. The Egyptian vulture uses stones to break into its favorite food, ostrich eggs. Birds can have very fussy tastes. Bat hawks, for example, only eat bats. Some eagles eat fish, while others prefer snakes.

? How do ospreys hunt?

Ospreys fly high above the water looking for fish. When they spot one, they dive and enter the water feet-first to catch it. Their toes have tiny sharp spikes for gripping slippery fish.

Osprey

❓ Which bird is a national symbol?

Eagles are the most powerful birds of prey and are often pictured on flags. The bald eagle is the national emblem of the USA, standing for strength and power.

Is it true?

The peregrine falcon can travel faster than an express train.

YES. When it spots a flying bird, the peregrine falcon folds its wings close to its body and dives at up to 220 mph.

Vultures

❓ Which birds are garbage collectors?

Vultures wait for creatures to die before rushing down to eat everything except the bones. They are very useful birds, getting rid of dead animals before they rot and spread disease.

❓ Which birds can be trained?

Hawks and falcons can be trained by people. Hawks fly fast and low over the ground when they hunt. A long time ago the goshawk used to be trained to catch food for people. It was known as the cook's bird.

 Amazing! The Andean condor from South America is the biggest bird of prey. It has a wingspan of over nine feet and it weighs up to 24 pounds.

Peregrine falcon on falconer's glove

137

? Which owl is as white as snow?

The snowy owl lives in the icy Arctic. The male's feathers are pure white so that it can't be seen against the snow when it hunts for hares and lemmings. It has feathers on its feet to help keep its toes warm.

Snowy owl

? Why do owls hoot?

Owls make sounds to communicate with each other in the dark. Different owls have different calls. They also use a wide range of sounds, from clicks to grunts to hisses. When courting, some owls actually sing to each other!

138

How many types of owl are there?

There are 133 different kinds of owl, most of which hunt at night. Their special soft feathers mean they fly silently through the dark. With huge eyes and excellent hearing, they can swoop down to take prey by surprise.

Barn owl

Amazing! When an owl eats its prey there are usually parts it cannot digest, such as claws, teeth, beaks and fur. These parts are made into balls called pellets and passed back out through the bird's mouth.

Is it true?
An eagle owl's ears are on top of its head.

NO. The tufts on top of its head may look like ears, but they are only long feathers. The owl's real ears are under the feathers at the sides of its head.

Eagle owl

? Why do birds have feathers?

Birds have three different kinds of feathers: down to keep warm; body feathers to cover and protect; and flight feathers. Baby birds have down feathers and can't fly until they've grown all their flight feathers.

Albatross chick

Is it true?
All flamingos are pink.

NO. In the wild, flamingos are generally pink. Color from the food is absorbed and passes to the feathers. But in captivity, their feathers can turn white if they have a change of diet.

Close-up of water on feathers

? How do birds keep clean?

All birds comb, or preen, their feathers with their beaks and claws. Love birds preen each other. Most birds also spread oil on their feathers from a gland above the tail, which keeps them waterproof.

Why are some feathers bright and others dull?

Many woodland birds, such as the tawny frogmouth, have dull feathers so that they can blend in with their background and keep safe. Male birds are often more brightly colored to attract a mate.

Tawny frogmouth and chick

Amazing!

Most birds have over 1,000 feathers and some birds have an enormous number. Swans have about 25,000 feathers – more than almost any other bird!

? How do birds fly?

Birds need to be light but strong to fly. They flap their wings to take off and fly higher in air. As the wing flaps down, the flight feathers close against the air, which pushes the bird up and forward.

Reed warbler

? What has to run to take off?

Swans are too big and heavy to leap into the air. Instead they have to run along the surface of the water, flapping their powerful wings to get enough speed to take off.

Swan

Amazing!

Big seabirds glide on air currents, sometimes not landing for weeks. Other birds can stay in the air for months, while swifts can spend years in the air, only landing to nest and mate.

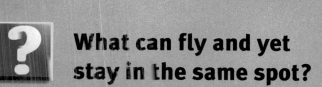

Kestrel

What can fly and yet stay in the same spot?

Kestrels are experts at hovering. They fly into the wind and beat their wings very quickly. This lets them stay in the same position as they search for prey below.

Is it true?

Birds can only fly forwards.

NO. Hummingbirds are special. They can fly forwards, sideways, backwards and hover on the spot by flapping their wings very quickly!

Whose beak can hold more than its stomach?

A pelican has a beak with a stretchy pouch which can hold far more fish than its stomach! It scoops fish from the water using its beak like a fishing net.

Amazing!
A woodpecker uses its unusual beak to drill for insects, to make holes in dying trees to use as nests, and to hammer on a tree to mark its territory.

❓ Why do birds have beaks?

Birds use their beaks to catch and hold food, to make nests and to preen themselves. They have different beaks because they eat different food. The toucan uses its enormous beak to pull fruits from delicate branches.

Toucan

Is it true?

Birds have teeth.

NO. Birds cannot chew, so they grind food up with a gizzard inside their bodies, and sometimes by swallowing small stones too.

Yellow-headed parrot

❓ What climbs with its beak?

Parrots usually live in big noisy groups in tropical forests. They have short, curved powerful beaks for cracking nuts and seeds. Some parrots have beaks so strong that they can even use them to pull themselves up trees.

145

Why do ducks have webbed feet?

Water birds have skin between their toes. Their feet are like paddles, helping them move easily through the water. They can also walk on mud without sinking in.

Amazing! Jacanas are water birds that live in tropical places. Their very long toes allow them to step on water plants without sinking. They are sometimes called 'lily-trotters'.

African jacana

Redhead duck

Is it true?
Birds stand on one leg when they've hurt their foot.

NO. When a bird stands on one leg, it is keeping the other foot warm, tucked up under its feathers.

Heron

? What has legs like stilts?

Herons and storks have very long legs which look like stilts. They are ideal for standing or wading in shallow water, where the birds use their long beaks to catch fish and frogs.

Budgerigar

? Why don't birds fall when they sleep?

Birds have a long tendon attached to each toe. When they rest on branches or another perch, they bend their legs and their toes lock around the perch.

❓ What hangs upside down to court?

When the male bird of paradise wants to attract a female it hangs upside down to show off its beautiful tail. Females and chicks are often dull compared to males so that they can remain safely hidden in the trees.

Male blue bird of paradise

Amazing! Great crested grebes dance on the water in front of each other for several weeks before they finally mate and pair for life. They can perform four separate complicated dance routines.

What hypnotizes with its 'eyes'?

The male peacock has a fan made of beautiful jeweled feathers. The 'eyes' on the feathers fascinate its mate, the peahen. By looking at them, she can tell that he is a healthy male to choose.

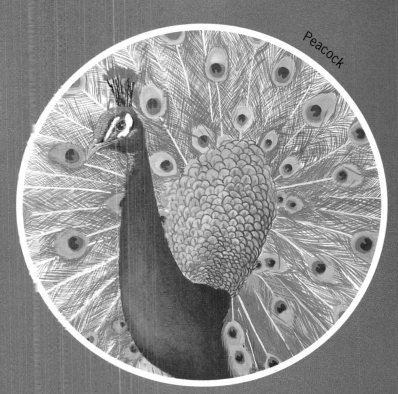
Peacock

Is it true?

Birds stay with a mate for only one season.

NO. Some birds, including swans, gannets and golden eagles, find a mate and stay with that same bird for the rest of their lives.

What attracts its mate with a red balloon?

The male frigate bird has a bright red pouch under his chin. When he wants to find a mate, he puffs it out like a balloon. If the female is impressed, she rubs her head against the pouch.

Frigate birds

Why do birds build nests?

Most birds build nests to hide their eggs and to keep their young warm and safe from enemies. Colonies of weaver birds often build several nests in the same tree.

Black-headed weaver birds

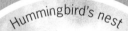
Hummingbird's nest

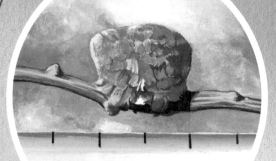

Amazing! Some nests are huge. An eagle's nest or eyrie is so big that you could lie down in it! Some birds, such as the hummingbird, make tiny nests. The bee hummingbird's nest is the same size as a thimble.

Thrushes

Why do birds sit on their eggs?

Birds sit on their eggs to keep them warm while the baby birds inside grow. If the eggs get cold, the babies inside will die, so birds don't leave their eggs alone for long.

Is it true?

Nests are birds' homes where they sleep at night.

NO. Birds only use nests for laying eggs and raising their chicks. They rest at night in hedges, trees or holes.

? Do birds' eggs all look the same?

Birds' eggs are often colored or patterned for camouflage. The guillemot's eggs are also an unusual shape. They are pointed at one end so that if nudged, they spin in a circle instead of rolling off a cliff.

What do newly hatched birds look like?

The young of tree-nesting birds are naked and blind at first. Their parents have to look after them, and they are always hungry! They open their beaks wide and call loudly, which forces the parents to feed them.

Looking down on baby birds

Amazing!
The hummingbird lays the world's smallest eggs. Each is only the size of your fingernail. Compared to this, an ostrich egg is huge, and thousands of times heavier.

Grebe with young

What sits on its mother's back?
Baby grebes can swim soon after they hatch. When they get cold or tired, they sit on their mother's back to warm up and have a rest.

Ostriches and chicks

❓ Which father sits on his eggs until they hatch?

The male ostrich makes eggs with up to twelve different females. The females all lay their eggs in same nest. The male then sits on them himself until they hatch. Many types of male bird, including pigeons, take it in turns with the female to sit on the eggs.

 Is it true?
A duckling could mistake you for its mother.

YES. A duckling thinks that the first creature it sees after hatching is its mother. If you were around, that would be you!

153

Which bird calls to find its nest?

When a male gannet has caught fish for his mate and young, he must call out and wait for the female's reply before he can find them amongst all the other gannets.

Gannets

Why do birds sing?

Birds sing most of all during the breeding season. A male bird sings to attract a mate, or to tell other birds to keep away from his territory. Males and females also call to warn other birds that an enemy is near, such as a cat or a human.

Magpie lark

Which birds copy sounds?

Some birds are natural mimics. This means they can copy sounds, such as the telephone ringing or even human speech. The mynah bird used to be popular as a caged pet because of this talent. Australian lyrebirds can even imitate a chainsaw!

Amazing! The African grey parrot is a real chatterbox. It can learn up to 800 different words, but it doesn't know what they mean!

Superb lyrebird

Is it true?
Birds can sing very high notes.

YES. Many birds can sing notes too high for us to hear! There is a wide range of beautiful birdsong, full of high and low notes.

Pigeon

? Which bird finds its way home?

Pigeons have a great sense of direction. Scientists think they use the position of the Sun, Moon and stars, the Earth's magnetic pull and landmarks. People race pigeons as a hobby, because they usually find their way home safely.

Snow geese

Amazing! The Arctic tern travels right across the Earth, from the Arctic to Antarctica and back again each year. That's a round trip of 22,000 miles. It keeps up its energy by eating fish as it flies.

Is it true?

Migrating birds must eat as they travel.

NO. Many kinds of birds do not eat during their migration. Instead they eat large amounts of food before they leave in order to survive the trip.

Which birds fly in a 'V' pattern?

Geese migrate in groups like this, or they fly together in long chains. The younger birds learn which way to go by following the older birds in front.

Do migrating birds remember the way?

Some migrating birds use familiar landmarks such as islands or mountains to find their way. Swifts often fly from the other side of the world back to the same nest each year.

Swift

? What was a dodo?

Have you heard the expression 'as dead as a dodo'? Dodos were strange-looking, heavy birds that could not fly. They lived on islands in the Indian Ocean until sailors hunted the very last one. Sadly, they have been extinct since 1800.

Dodo

Kiwi

? What has invisible wings?

Kiwis are flightless birds whose wings are so tiny that you cannot see them. They have long whiskers, no tail and a good sense of smell. They hunt at night for worms and insects.

? Which bird 'flies' underwater?

Penguins are water birds which cannot fly. They live in the chilly Antarctic. They slide on snow and ice using their bellies as toboggans. But in water they are very graceful, using their wings as flippers as they swim along catching fish.

Is it true?

Penguins argue with their wings.

YES. Penguins live close together. When they squabble with each other, they flap their wings and jab their beaks to help make their point!

King penguins

Amazing! Ostriches cannot fly, but they can run very quickly indeed. The African ostrich can sprint along at 40 mph! They live in dry grasslands and may have to travel a long way for food.

CHAPTER SIX

WILD CATS

AND OTHER DANGEROUS PREDATORS

Grizzly bear

What do cats, dogs and bears have in common?

They are all mammals. This means that they are covered with cosy fur and feed their young with mother's milk. Cats, dogs and bears are also all carnivores, which means they eat meat. To do this, they have special sharp, pointy teeth, called canines.

Is it true?
Cats, dogs and bears are the only carnivores in the world.

NO. Many other mammals, such as hyenas, weasels, raccoons and humans eat meat. So do other animals – birds of prey, some reptiles and sharks in the sea.

Great white shark

Amazing! There were mammals around at the same time as the dinosaurs. Just like dinosaurs, some were carnivorous (meat-eating), such as Zalambdalestes, and some were herbivores (vegetarians).

What is a Tasmanian devil?

The Tasmanian devil lives in Tasmania, an island south of mainland Australia, and belongs to the same mammal family as kangaroos, carrying its babies in a pouch on its tummy. It's small, ferocious, and can defend itself well against other predators.

Tasmanian devil

Are hyenas dogs?

No, though they look quite similar. Hyenas hunt in packs like dogs, but they have four toes per foot, whereas dogs have five on their front paws. Hyenas are not cats either, but are closely related.

163

Do dogs ever kill people?

The gray wolf is one member of the dog family that is powerful enough to kill a person. There have been tales of gray wolf attacks in Europe and Asia. The worst story dates back to 1948, when a pack appeared in Darovskoye, Russia. Witnesses said the wolves killed 40 children and then disappeared, probably with very full tummies!

Amazing!

Stories such as Goldilocks, Little Red Riding Hood and Peter and the Wolf were probably made up to stop children from wandering off into places where there were dangerous bears and wolves.

Gray wolves

Indian tiger

Is it true?

Foxes are more dangerous than wolves.

YES. Although foxes are too small to attack a person, they are far more dangerous because they can carry a deadly disease called rabies. A bite from a rabid fox could mean death for the victim unless he or she reaches a doctor in time to be given anti-rabies medicine.

When do bears eat people?

When they're very, very hungry polar bears! Bears usually avoid people, but occasionally young male polar bears attack people, during especially harsh winters.

Grizzly bear

Bear Country

Danger do not Approach or Feed

Are there killer cats?

Cougars, jaguars and leopards have all killed people, but the serious maneaters are lions and tigers. One tigress was said to gobble up 436 people in just eight years!

Amazing!
Lions doze for up to 20 hours a day. They save all their energy for hunting and fighting.

? Do lions hunt alone?

Most cats are loners, but lions hunt as a team with the rest of their pride (family group). Male lions are too easy to spot with their huge flowing manes, so usually the females hunt. Still, the male lions get to dig into their share first.

Lioness

Lion

? How loud is a lion's roar?

Very loud! On a still day, and it usually is quite still in Africa, a lion's roar can be heard three miles away. Lions roar to show other lions how strong they are, and to communicate with other members of the pride.

Is it true?
Only lions have manes.

YES AND NO. Normally, only male lions have manes. A mane makes them look bigger and scar er, and the extra fur protects their neck in a fight. Lionesses do not usually have manes, but people studying lions in Africa have come across a few females with mini manes of their own!

Wildebeest

Lion cubs

Do lion cubs look like their parents?

Adult lions have plain, sandy-colored fur, but their cubs have spots on their coats. This might be camouflage, to make them difficult to see when their mother has to leave them alone and go off hunting.

? Can any animal outrun a cheetah?

Over short distances, the cheetah tops 60 miles per hour, and no animal can beat that. Cheetahs reach such high speeds partly because their dog-like claws work like running shoes and give them a good grip. But the speed king soon runs out of puff. If an impala keeps ahead for more than 550 yards, its life is saved – at least this time!

Cheetah

Impala

 Amazing! The average cheetah hunt is over in seconds! A cheetah may spend hours lazing about lying in wait, but it normally runs down its prey within 300 yards. It takes the cat less than 20 seconds to catch its meal!

How does the cheetah kill its prey?

The cheetah lives on the African grasslands. It usually chases animals such as antelopes, gazelles or even ostriches. When it catches up with its fast-running prey, it fells and kills it by clamping its strong jaws on to its neck.

Cheetah with prey

Is it true?
Cheetahs are spotted all over.

NO. The cheetah is mostly spotted, but its tail is striped. And the king cheetah, which is extremely rare, has stripes on its back where the spots have joined up.

Where do cheetah cubs live?
Cheetah mothers don't have a permanent den. Instead, they move their cubs around a couple of times each week. This stops other big cats finding and preying on them.

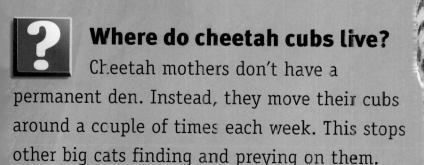
Cheetah and cub

169

Is it true?

Tigers don't attack a victim which looks them in the eye.

YES. Tigers usually attack from behind. In Southeast Asia, people sometimes wear masks that act as fake faces, on the backs of their heads.

Who's the biggest cat of all?

The Siberian tiger can reach a record-breaking eleven feet long – that's about six times longer than a pet cat. This tiger is very rare and lives in the mountains of northern China and Russia. Its long, off-white, striped fur keeps it warm and hidden in the snow.

Siberian tiger

170

How big is a tiger's paw?

Huge – almost as big as a grown-up's head! Even a gentle swipe of its paw would easily knock you off your feet.

Amazing! The cub of a male tiger and a female lion is called a tigon. Lions and tigers are so closely related that they have been bred together in zoos. Ligers are the cubs of a female tiger and a male lion.

 ## How many tigers are there?

There are five main types of tiger – the Siberian, South Chinese, Sumatran, Indochinese and Indian. The number of tigers has fallen faster than for any other cat. There are fewer than 5,000 in the world today.

Caspian tiger (probably extinct)

Which leopard has lost its spots?

The black panther, which is really a type of leopard! But if you were brave, or foolish, enough to get close to a panther, you'd see faint spots in its fur.

Leopard

Who hides in the trees?

Lots of spotted cats, including leopards and jaguars, hide in the trees to take a catnap or lie in wait for their prey. The dappled light through the leaves makes everything look spotted, so their coats are the perfect camouflage.

Leopard

Who hides a feast in the trees?

Sometimes leopards kill such big prey, that they can't eat it all in one go. Leopards can drag a whole deer up into the branches of a tree, safe from jackals and hyenas, which can't climb up and steal it!

 Amazing! The snow leopard is a champion long-jumper! This rare big cat can clear a 50 foot wide ditch – that's over one and a half times further than the human long-jump record.

 Is it true?
All cats hate the water.

NO. Quite a few types of cat enjoy a swim. Jaguars in the South American rainforests often bathe in the River Amazon. They love to snack on river turtles and sometimes even kill crocodiles!

Jaguar swimming

? How can you tell small cats from big?

Most big cats – lions, tigers, jaguars and leopards – roar. Small cats can only purr. There are lots of types of small cat, all over the world. They include the pet-cat-sized leopard cat of southern Asia, and the jaguarundi and ocelot, which both live in North and South America.

Caracal

European wild cat

 Amazing! Some cats wear slippers. The sand cat lives in the scorching Sahara Desert in Africa. It has special, thick pads on its paws to stop them from being burnt on the hot sand during the day.

Caracal

? Which cat barks?

The caracal sounds more like a dog than a cat, because it barks when it wants to call its mate. It also has tall, tufted ears, a short tail and can even be trained as a hunting pet. It is famous for leaping to catch birds in mid-air.

Jaguar

Ocelot

Jaguarundi

Leopard cat

European wild cat

Which cat has the most kittens?

Most small cats have between one and four kittens at a time, but the European wild cat has litters of as many as eight kittens! This champion breeder is found all over mainland Europe and also lives in the Highlands of northern Scotland.

Is it true?
Wild cats can breed with pet cats.

YES. But many pet cats are too scared to let their wild cousins get close enough! European wild cats often breed with pet cats or strays. The pedigree Bengal is a cross between a leopard cat and a tabby.

Do hyenas laugh?

The spotted, or laughing, hyena has two different calls. One sounds like a laugh, but the other sounds more like a wail. This hyena is very daring. It has attacked sleeping people and has even carried off young children!

 Amazing! Hyenas work as refuse collectors. Hyenas are scavengers – they will eat just about anything. In some African villages hyenas are sometimes allowed in to clear the garbage.

Spotted hyenas

 Is it true?
All hyenas have manes.

NO. Spotted hyenas don't, but striped hyenas and brown hyenas do. They have scruffy-looking hair sticking up around their head and even down their back.

Do hyena cubs get on together?

Hyena cubs play with each other to practice the skills they'll need as adults, but they don't really get on. Twins fight over food, and sometimes, the weaker twin slowly starves to death.

Hyena cubs

Vultures

Lioness with prey

Do hyenas hunt?

Spotted hyenas do, but other hyenas prefer other animals to do the work for them! Most hyenas feed mainly on carrion, which is a bigger hunter's leftovers. When they do hunt for themselves, hyenas go for wildebeest or zebra, or they steal a goat or cow from the local farmer.

? How do dogs hunt?

Many dogs, including African wild dogs, hunt in groups called packs. First they spread out, so they have a good view of the landscape, then they close in on their prey. They keep in contact with barks and body language.

African wild dogs

Warthog

? Do dogs use babysitters?

Yes! Jackals in particular live in very close-knit family groups. They share all the jobs. Sometimes a young female jackal is picked to stay at home looking after the cubs while all the other mothers go out hunting.

Is it true?

Dogs have five toes on each front paw.

YES. But the African wild dog is the one exception. This fierce hunter is missing a toe on each front foot.

African wild dog pups

Amazing! Dogs can't sweat! Unlike you, dogs don't have sweat glands, so they can't lose heat through their skin. They pant when they get hot, to let heat escape from their bodies.

Saint Bernard

? What do pups eat?

Newborn wild pups live off mother's milk. Soon, their mum brings them meat. She chews it for them, until they're a bit bigger. Finally at four months old, the pups are old enough to join in the hunt.

? What changes its coat in the winter?

The Arctic fox lives in the far North. In the summer, when flowers are in bloom, its fur is reddish brown. During the icy winter, it turns snowy-white for camouflage.

Arctic fox

 Is it true?

Fennec foxes have huge ears.

YES. In fact, they're six inches long! Fennecs hunt at night so they need good hearing to find prey. Big ears also help their body heat to escape.

Who's at home in the city?

Fantastic Mr Fox! The red fox is just as happy in the town as in the countryside. During the night, it goes through trash cans looking for tasty morsels or catches rats.

Gray fox

City foxes

Amazing!

The gray fox can climb trees! From high in the branches, the fox gets a good lookout for rabbits and mice. It can also grab a fast-food snack, such as fruit or an egg from a nest.

Who won the race, the fox or the hare?

Foxes only catch hares by sneaking up on them without being seen. If the hare hears or sees the fox, it dashes off. Hares can outrun foxes, and both animals know it!

181

Which is the biggest dog?

The gray wolf is biggest wild dog and the most powerful. Males can be as long as six feet and weigh up to 175 pounds, as much as four six-year-old children! Some gray wolves have brown, red or black coats.

Gray wolf

 Amazing! Except for the African wild dog, all pet dogs are descended from a wolf-like ancestor, which appeared about one million years ago.

Do wolves howl at the Moon?

Wolves howl whether the Moon's out or not. They use their powerful voices to tell other packs of wolves to stay away, and to talk to members of their own pack, especially when they have spread out to hunt.

Is it true?
You should never try to out-stare a wolf.

NO. You should if you're a musk ox. Wolves usually hunt by picking off young or sick members of a group of grazing animals. Musk oxen try to stop this happening by huddling in a tight circle. Faced with a wall of horns, the Arctic wolves can't pick off any individual oxen.

Which wolf walks on stilts?

The maned wolf is the tallest wild dog. Its legs are longer than the length of its body! The maned wolf lives in the grasslands of South America. Its stilts give it a good view over the tall Pampas grasses.

Maned wolf

Which is the biggest bear?

The powerful polar bear weighs in at 1,320 pounds, which makes it about ten times heavier than an adult person, and the biggest of all meat-eating land mammals. Adult bears snack on fish and seals, but they have even been spotted guzzling down fat beluga whales that weigh as much as themselves!

Polar bear

Amazing! Polar bears cover their nose with their paw when they hunt. Although their fur is white, their noses are black and easy to spot in the snow. By covering its nose, the polar bear makes sure that its whole body is camouflaged against the snowy Arctic landscape.

Polar bear cubs

? Which cubs drink the creamiest milk?

Newborn polar bear cubs are tiny. They need to fatten up quickly to survive the cold. Luckily, their mother's milk is thick and creamy, and about half of it is pure fat.

? Can bears walk on water?

They can when it's frozen! Polar bears roam across northern Europe, northern Asia and North America. If the Arctic Ocean isn't frozen they swim, protected by thick fur and fat!

 Is it true?
Polar bears poisoned Arctic explorers.

YES. Polar bears' livers contain a lot of Vitamin A. In small doses, this is fine for humans, but when hungry explorers ate the livers, they were poisoned.

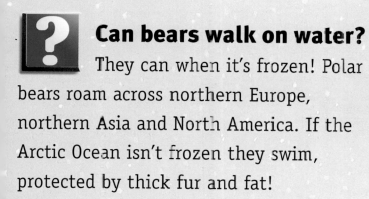

Which bear fishes for its supper?

The brown bear is a top angler. It knows just the time of year that delicious salmon head upriver to lay their eggs. The bear catches the fish with a quick swipe of the paw, or it waits until the salmon leap up mini waterfalls, and become tired.

Brown bear

Brown bear cub

When do bears climb trees?

When they want to escape danger. Black bears are expert climbers even as grown-ups. Brown bears only climb trees when they are cubs, usually to escape from adult brown bears, who are trying to eat them!

Amazing! The American black bear is one of the world's champion snoozers. Its winter sleep, or hibernation, lasts for seven months – over half of the year!

Is it true?
Koalas are bears.

NO. Although we call them koala bears, koalas are really marsupials, which means they have pouches like kangaroos. Pandas aren't bears either. They're more closely related to raccoons.

Do all bears eat meat?

Even meat-eating bears sometimes like a change of diet. Polar bears snack on seaweed and berries when seals are scarce. Brown and black bears love honey, but collecting it is a very risky business. They often come away from the hive with a stung nose!

Giant panda

American national park

? Where can you see bears close-up?

National parks give bears a home where they're safe from hunters. If you visit one of these nature reserves, remember that bears are wild and can be dangerous to humans.

Huskies pulling sled

Amazing!

Pet owners live longer! Lots of people choose to share their lives with pet cats and dogs, the cousins of wild lions and wolves. Stroking an animal feels good and helps pet owners to relax. Scientists think this may explain why they live longer.

How do dogs help people?

Lots of dogs work for us. Huskies pull people around in the icy Arctic. Other dogs' jobs include mountain rescue, herding sheep and helping blind and deaf people. The skills which wild dogs use to hunt, such as working as a team and having superb senses, make them ideal for these tasks.

Is it true?
Humans are the most dangerous animals on Earth.

YES. Animals which attack humans are extremely rare, but we have hunted animals for fur, and destroyed their habitats. That's why so many creatures are in danger of dying out.

Where can you see big cats close-up?

In a zoo. Some people think it's cruel to keep animals away from the wild. Other people say that zoos are useful for breeding rare cats and teaching us about them.

Lions in zoo

CHAPTER SEVEN

WHALES

AND OTHER SEA MAMMALS

Dugong

What are sea mammals?

Sea mammals spend most of their lives in or near the sea. There are three groups of sea mammals. Whales and dolphins are called cetaceans. Seals and walruses are called pinnipeds. Manatees and dugongs are called sirenians.

 Amazing! There are well over 10 million crabeater seals living in the icy Antarctic. Seals are found in many parts of the world, but the southern crabeaters are the most common type of seal on Earth.

Blue whale

192

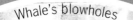
Whale's blowholes

Which special features help whales live in the sea?

A whale's body is designed for swimming. It has a smooth, streamlined shape for pushing through the water, and blowholes for breathing on top of its head.

Which is the biggest sea mammal?

The huge blue whale is the biggest mammal in the sea. In fact, it's the biggest animal that has ever lived. It can grow more than 100 feet long and weigh as much as 130 tons.

Is it true?
Whales once lived on land.

YES. The ancestors of today's whales once lived on land. About 50 million years ago, they went into the sea to look for food and their bodies adapted to life in the water.

Amazing! Whales have a thick layer of fat, called blubber, under their skins. This keeps them warm in the cold sea. At about 20 inches, the bowhead whale has the thickest blubber.

? Do all whales have teeth?

Some whales have long, tough bristles, called baleen, hanging down inside their mouths, instead of teeth. They don't chew their food, but sieve it from the water through the baleen.

Baleen whale

Is it true?
A whale uses its blowhole as a nose.

YES. Like all mammals, whales must breathe air to stay alive. Instead of nostrils, they have a blowhole on top of the head.

Close up of barnacles

Barnacles

What has tiny shellfish on its back?

Some whales have tons of tiny shellfish growing on their backs. The shellfish are called barnacles. They need to have a solid surface to glue their shells on to. Any rock, ship or passing whale will do.

Dolphin

? **What's the difference between whales and dolphins?**

Strictly speaking, dolphins are small whales with sharp, pointed teeth for catching food. Dolphins live in seas all over the world. The biggest dolphin is the killer whale.

195

What do walruses use their tusks for?

A walrus uses its long tusks to chip shellfish from rocks and break breathing holes in the ice. The males also use their tusks to fight off rivals and attract a mate.

Walruses

Hooded seal

Which seal blows up balloons?

To attract a mate or scare off a rival, a male hooded seal blows air into its nose! It can inflate the lining of one of its nostrils so that it looks like a big, red balloon.

Is it true?

Seals cry when they are sad.

NO. Seals sometimes look as if they're crying, but it's not because they're sad. The tears keep their eyes moist and clean. In the sea, they get washed away. On land, they trickle down their cheeks.

Weddell seal

Which seals live at the ends of the Earth?

Weddell seals live in the far south, on ice-covered islands off the coast of freezing Antarctica. Ringed seals live in the Arctic, at the other end of the world. They've been found as far north as the North Pole.

Amazing! In hot weather, some seals and sealions flip tiny pebbles and sand on to their backs with their flippers. This helps to keep them cool, and it also scratches them if their skin is feeling itchy.

❓ Where do manatees and dugongs live?

Manatees and dugongs live in tropical rivers and in warm, shallow water near the coast, in tropical seas. They are sometimes called 'sea cows' or 'sea pigs' because of their large, lumbering shapes.

Sea cow

Amazing! Florida manatees don't have homes on land, so they sleep on the seabed. They live off the southeastern coast of the United States. These manatees have to come to the surface every ten minutes to breathe the air which keeps them alive.

Is it true?
You can tell a dugong's age from its tusks.

YES. To tell a dugong's age, you need to count the growth rings in its tusks. In the wild, dugongs can live for between 60 and 70 years.

How can you tell manatees and dugongs apart?

You can tell manatees and dugongs apart by the shape of their tails. A manatee's tail has rounded tips. A dugong's tail has pointed tips, like a dolphin's tail.

Dugong

Manatee

Dugong

Which sea mammals are vegetarians?

Only manatees and dugongs are vegetarians. They feed on sea grasses and other sea plants. They use their bristly lips for pulling up plants. Dugongs also dig up roots from the seabed using their horseshoe-shaped snouts. All other sea mammals eat meat, or other creatures of some kind.

Which sea mammal can swim the fastest?

The fastest sea mammal in the world is the killer whale. With its streamlined body and powerful tail, it can speed through the water at up to 35 mph. That's more than six times faster than the quickest human swimmers.

Killer whales

Is it true?
Spinner dolphins spin like tops in the air.

YES. Spinner dolphins are easy to recognize. They can leap out of the water, high into the air, then spin around quickly like tops. These amazing acrobats live near the coast in warm seas.

Sea lion

Which is the speediest seal?

The fastest seal in the sea is the California sea lion, with a top speed of 25 mph. The fastest on land is the crabeater seal, reaching 12 mph over snow and ice.

Amazing!

Some sea mammals can hold their breath for almost two hours before they have to come to the surface for air. Most humans can only hold their breath for a minute or so.

Sperm whale

Giant squid

What is one of the deepest divers?

Sperm whales dive over a mile after their food. One sperm whale was even found with two deep-sea sharks in its stomach. It must have dived to two miles to catch them.

Which whales turn somersaults in the air?

Humpback whales are very athletic. Even though the whales may weigh 65 tons, they can leap high into the air and come crashing down into the water on their backs. They can even turn somersaults in the air.

Humpback whale

Amazing! In the Arctic and Antarctic, seals dive under the ice to search for food. They can hold their breath for up to 30 minutes before they need to come up for air, so they chew breathing holes in the ice with their strong front teeth.

Which sea mammals walk with their teeth?

A walrus's tusks are actually its two upper teeth. They grow up to three feet long. The walrus uses its tusks to pull itself out of the sea and drag itself across the land.

Walrus

Gray whale

 Which sea mammals make the longest journey?

Gray whales spend the summers feeding in the Arctic. In winter, they swim to the coast of Mexico to breed. They swim back north again in the spring, a round trip of about 12,500 miles.

 Is it true?
Whales slap their tails against the sea surface because they're angry.

NO. Some whales slap their huge tails down on the water but it's not because they're angry. This is called 'lobtailing' and it's probably a signal to other whales.

Which are the most intelligent sea mammals?

Dolphins are quick to learn tricks and remember instructions. This makes them very popular with people. They are also friendly and sociable. Many dolphins live in large groups. They play and hunt for food together.

Which seal has a huge nose?

The male northern elephant seal gets its name from its very long nose, which normally hangs down over its mouth. It can inflate its nose, like a balloon, to attract a mate.

Northern elephant seal

NO. Beluga whales whistle and chirp just like singing birds, such as canaries. In fact, they make so much noise, they're nicknamed 'sea canaries'. Adult belugas have pure white skin.

Dolphin

Humpback whales

Amazing! Blue whales' voices are louder than the sound of a jet plane taking off, and can be heard over 300 miles away. As well as being the biggest animals, blue whales are the noisiest creatures in the world!

Why do whales sing to each other?

Whales build sounds into 'songs' which can last for ten minutes or more. The whales sing to keep in touch with each other, to find a mate and to frighten off rivals.

Baleen

? Which whale has the longest 'teeth'?

All of the great whales, such as the blue whale have hundreds of bony baleen, which they use to sieve food from the water. The Bowhead whale's baleen are up to 13 feet long.

Leopard seal

Is it true?
Leopard seals are fussy eaters.

NO. Leopard seals eat almost anything, including penguins, sea birds, fish, squid, seal pups, and even duck-billed platypuses!

? How do leopard seals catch their prey?

Leopard seals mainly eat penguins. To catch them, the seals build up speed in the water, then launch themselves on to the ice. They have even been known to snap at human divers, probably because they mistake them for penguins.

Blue whale

Which sea mammal has the biggest appetite?

Blue whales have massive appetites. In spring and summer, they eat up to four tons of krill (tiny, shrimp-like creatures) each day. That's about five times as much food as you eat each year!

Amazing! Whales and dolphins can shut off their windpipes when they're underwater. They do this when they're feeding. It stops water from passing into their lungs and making them choke.

What finds food with its whiskers?

A walrus has a thick moustache of about 600 whiskers around its snout. It uses them to feel for shellfish, sea urchins, fish and crabs on the seabed.

Walrus

Which sea mammals use fishing nets?

Humpbacks, killer whales and dolphins swim around shoals of fish, blowing bubbles from their blowholes. Then they swim and gobble the trapped fish up!

 Amazing! Some seals swallow stones and pebbles. No one knows exactly why. Perhaps, like some birds which do the same, they swallow the stones to help grind up their food, or maybe they stop hunger pangs.

Is it true?

Dolphins use echo-location to find food.

YES. Dolphins use sound to find food underwater. They make clicking sounds which are too high-pitched for human ears to hear. If the sounds hit a solid object, like a fish, they send back echoes. From the echoes, the dolphins can tell what's nearby.

Humpback whale

Dolphins hunting fish

? What uses a ceiling of water to catch fish?

When dolphins are hunting for anchovy, they herd the fish towards the surface of the water, giving them one less direction of escape. They also make loud noises, which might confuse the fish, making them easier to catch.

Amazing! Walruses get sunburnt. Walruses are usually brown. But in strong sun, their blood flows to the skin's surface to soak up the heat. This can turn the walruses' skin a bright shade of pink.

Killer whales

How can you tell humpback whales apart?

Humpback whales have special black and white markings under their tails. Each whale has its own particular pattern which can be used to tell the whales apart. These markings are unique to each whale, just like one person's fingerprints are never the same as anybody else's.

Humpback whale

? Why are killer whales black and white?

The killer whale's black and white coloring looks very striking, but it could be camouflage. It might help to hide the whale among the light and shade near the water surface, so it can take fish and seals by surprise.

Is it true?
Some porpoises wear spectacles.

NO. Spectacled porpoises don't wear real glasses but they have black spectacle-like markings around their eyes. These porpoises live in the Atlantic Ocean.

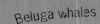
Beluga whales

? Which whales change color as they grow up?

Beluga whales live in the Arctic Ocean. New-born beluga babies are reddish-brown in color. After about a year, their skin changes color to gray. When they're five years old, they turn pure white.

Amazing! Every year, a herd of about 1.5 million fur seals gather on the Pribilof Islands in Alaska to breed. What a squash!

? Which are the biggest sea mammal babies?

When a baby blue whale is born, it weighs between two and three tons. It drinks about 105 pints of its mother's milk a day, and by seven months old, it weighs 20 tons!

Blue whale and calf

? Which sea mammals live in a pod?

Some dolphins live in family groups called pods. A pod may be hundreds of dolphins strong. The dolphins help each other out. If one of them is ill, for example, the others look after it, by pushing it to the surface so that it can breathe.

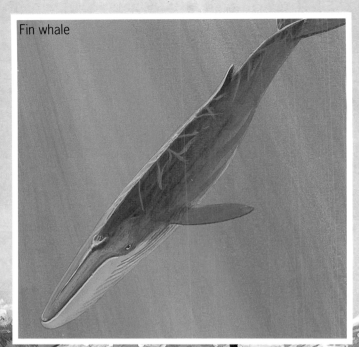
Fin whale

? Which sea mammals live the longest?

Whales and dolphins have long lives. Fin whales probably live the longest, between 90 and 100 years. The Baird's beaked whale is close behind. It can live for up to 80 years.

Is it true?
Baby whales and dolphins are born head first.

NO. A baby whale or dolphin is born tail first. Otherwise it might drown. Its mother pushes it to the surface so that it can take its first breath.

Pod of dolphins

Amazing! Scientists think that the closest relatives of manatees and dugongs may be elephants! After all, they're all large and lumbering, they're all grayish in color and they all eat plants. But they drifted apart millions of years ago.

Dugongs

Pilot whales

? Why do whales get stranded on the beach?

Groups of whales sometimes get stranded on the shore. If they can't return to the sea, they die. No one knows why this happens. It may be because they're ill, or get confused and lose their way.

 Is it true?
Narwhals use their tusks for jousting.

YES. Only male narwhals grow long, spiraling tusks. It is thought that they may use their tusks as jousting weapons to fight off rival narwhals for a mate.

Narwhals

? Do unicorns really exist?

Not on land, but people used to hunt narwhals, a type of whale, and sell their tusks as unicorn horns. The tusk is the narwhal's tooth. It grows up to eight feet long.

? Which sea mammals did sailors mistake for mermaids?

The legend of the mysterious mermaid may have started with a dugong. Close-up, dugongs don't look anything like mermaids, but from a distance, and in a sea mist, they do look a bit like human shapes, complete with fish-like tails.

? Which seal pups were hunted for their coats?

Harp seal pups are born with soft, white fur coats. They lose these after a month and grow dark coats like adult seals. In the past, thousands of pups were killed for their fur.

Harp seal pup

Amazing! Steller's sea cows were huge dugongs that once lived in the Bering Sea. They were discovered in 1741. Just 30 years later, they were extinct because so many had been eaten by sailors.

Whale hunt

Why are sea mammals in danger?

People are very dangerous for sea mammals. They hunt seals and whales for their meat, fur and blubber, and they trap sea mammals, such as dolphins, in fishing nets. Many more mammals are poisoned by pollution, such as oil from tankers, which is dumped into the sea.

 ### Is it true?
Right whales are easy to hunt.

YES. Right whales were once the right whales to hunt. They swam slowly and floated on the surface when they were killed.

Gulf porpoises

 ## Which are the rarest sea mammals?

There are fewer than 600 Mediterranean monk seals left, but the rarest sea mammal is probably the Gulf porpoise. There may be only 50 left off the Californian coast.

Elephant seal

Amazing!

Most whales and dolphins are able to snooze for a few minutes while they're swimming or resting on the sea floor. But it's thought that the Dall's porpoise never goes to sleep at all.

? Which is the biggest seal?

Antarctic southern elephant seals are the biggest seals. Male seals grow up to 20 feet long, measure almost 13 feet around the middle and weigh in at about three tons.

Blue whale

Is it true?

Sperm whales have the heaviest mammal brains.

YES. A sperm whale's brain weighs up to 20 pounds. That's about six times heavier than a human brain! Luckily, the whale has a very large head to fit it in, which takes up about a third of its body.

Which whale is the tiniest?

The smallest whale is probably the Commerson's dolphin. This miniature mammal grows about one metre long. It would take about 3,000 dolphins to make up the weight of one blue whale.

Commerson's dolphin

Which whale has the tallest 'blow'?

The 'blow' is the spout of water you see when a whale breathes out. The gigantic blue whale has the tallest blow. It can reach a height of 40 feet, as high as six tall people. Each whale makes a different pattern as it blows.

CHAPTER EIGHT

GORILLAS

AND OTHER PRIMATES

Spider monkey

? How do you tell a monkey from an ape?

By looking at its bottom! If it has no tail, it's probably either a 'great ape' – a gorilla, chimp, orang-utan, or bonobo – or it might be a type of gibbon or 'lesser ape', such as the siamang. Except for a few out of over 100 types, monkeys do have tails. Monkeys and apes belong to a group of intelligent animals called primates.

Gorilla

 Amazing! You are a primate! Like all primates, you have forward-facing eyes, a big brain and hands that grip. Your genes (the instructions which tell your body what to be) are actually very similar to a chimp's genes.

Hedgehog

Experts used to say that the tree shrew was a primate, but really they're more similar to insect-eating creatures such as moles, shrews and hedgehogs.

Slender loris

Crowned lemur

❓ Are monkeys and apes the only primates?

Lemurs, bushbabies, lorises and tarsiers are all primitive primates. They have smaller brains than monkeys or apes and rely more on their sense of smell than sight.

Tarsier

Is it true?
Primates were around in dinosaur days.

YES People have found fossils of early, squirrel-sized primates that lived about 70 million years ago – about the same time that terrifying Tyrannosaurus rex roamed the land.

Which primates play in the snow?

Japanese macaques are sometimes called snow monkeys. They are found farther north than any other primate, except humans. For five months of the year, the mountains where they live are covered with snow. They grow an extra-thick winter coat and there are lots of hot springs, where they can take a steamy bath when they are feeling the chill.

 Amazing! Brazil, in South America, is home to about 50 types of primate, more than any other country. Most of Brazil is covered in rainforest, which makes the perfect home for a tree-loving primate.

Japanese macaques

Barbary macaque

? Which primates play on the rocks?

There are about 100 barbary macaques living on the Rock of Gibraltar, just off the southwest coast of Europe. They feed on grass, young leaves, spiders and treats from tourists.

Is it true?
Lemurs are found all over the world.

NO. Apart from in zoos, lemurs are only found on the islands of Madagascar and the Comoros, off the southeast coast of Africa.

Chacma baboon

? Which primates play in the sand?

In the Namib Desert, Africa, there's less than two inches of rainfall each year. The chacma baboons, which live there, eat wild figs for moisture, but often don't drink water for two or three months.

Which ape has the longest arms?

In relation to its overall size, the orang-utan has the biggest armspan. Its arms are three times as long as its body, which is just right for an animal that spends its life swinging from tree to tree! The name orang-utan is the Malay for 'man of the woods'.

Orang-utan

Is it true?
Gorillas in the wild are bigger than gorillas in zoos.

NO. Life in a zoo can make gorillas rather lazy and, sometimes, rather fat! The record-breaker was a male called N'gagi, who weighed in at a whopping 682 pounds. That's about the same as five adult humans!

Mandrill

Which is the most colorful monkey?

Male mandrills, which belong to the baboon family, have very brightly colored faces. Mandrills are also among the biggest monkeys, at about three feet tall, with a weight of about 44 pounds.

Mouse lemur

Amazing! The gorilla is the world's biggest ape. It is a tiny bit taller than a man, but usually about three times as heavy.

Which is the world's smallest primate?

The eastern brown mouse lemur of Madagascar is truly tiny. From the top of its head to its backside, it measures just over two inches. It could easily sit on your palm, if it wasn't so shy!

Gorilla

Is it true?
Gorillas are monster meat-eaters.

NO. Despite their enormous size, these gentle giants are vegetarians. They feed on fruits, roots and vegetables, especially delicious wild celery.

? **Where do gorillas sleep?**

It's not just birds that sleep in nests – huge gorillas do too! They bend branches in bushes and trees and make a cozy bed just above the ground. Sometimes they make a mini day nest, where they snatch a midday snooze.

Which gorillas go gray?

Adult male gorillas are called silverbacks, because of the silvery gray fur on their back and face. The silverback is the leader, who defends the troop.

Silverback gorilla

 Amazing! Gorillas use sign language! Wild gorillas communicate with grunts and body language. But a gorilla called Koko learned proper sign language, as used by people who can't speak or hear.

When is it rude to stare?

It's always rude to look straight at a gorilla. In gorilla language, staring means you're angry and looking for a fight. Sometimes, gorillas beat their chests when they're cross.

Proboscis monkey

Which monkey has a long nose?

The male proboscis monkey from Borneo has a giant nose, which sometimes droops down below its chin! No one really knows what it's for, but when the monkey makes its loud honking noise through the mangrove trees, its nose straightens out. Maybe the nose makes its call louder, like a bullhorn.

Which primate is always blushing?

The red uakari's face is bright scarlet in sunshine and completely bare of fur. This shy little monkey lives in the Amazon rainforest. It is an expert nutcracker and can even break hard Brazil nut shells.

Red uakari

Amazing! Primates go bald! Some chimps and bonobos in central Africa develop bald spots as they get older. The males lose their hair in a perfect triangle shape, and the females lose the lot!

Is it true?
Primates wear glasses.

NO. But the spectacled langur of Malaysia looks like it does. Most of its face is covered in dark fur but the monkey has white circles around its eyes that look like specs.

Which is the punkiest primate?

The cute cotton-top tamarin is the punk rocker of the primate world, with its mohican-style white crest. Lots of primates sport weird hairstyles. The tassel-eared marmoset has tufts of hair above its ears, while the emperor tamarin has a curly white moustache! These tiny monkeys are between five and 14 inches long, and live mostly in South American tropical forests.

Cotton-top tamarin

Tarsier

Amazing! The tarsier has enormous, goggly eyes. If you had eyes as large in relation to your head, they'd be as big as grapefruits!

Who hangs on for dear life?

The spectral tarsier of Indonesia spends the day sleeping, clinging tightly to a vertical branch. The tips of its fingers are like flattened, sticky pads, and they give it a good grip on its peculiar bed. They also come in handy when the tarsier is hunting for the grubs and insects that it likes to eat.

Is it true?
The aye-aye brings bad luck.

NO. But some people living on Madagascar think it does. They believe that if they see one and don't kill it, someone in their village will die. That's one of the reasons why this odd-looking primate is in danger of disappearing.

232

When do pottos play dead?

When a potto spots a predator (hunter), it sometimes pretends to be dead. It just lets go of its tree and drops to the forest floor. It has another form of defence, too. Its extra-thick neck protects it if it's snatched by a hungry predator.

Golden potto

Which primate has bat-like ears?

The aye-aye's ears are huge and give it amazing hearing. They help it to hear grubs gnawing away under the tree bark. The aye-aye also has a long middle finger, for winkling out its juicy dinner.

Aye-aye

What ate 500 figs in a single week?

All lemurs love to come across a tree of juicy figs, but one ruffed lemur once ate about 500 figs in a week. The greedy lemur defended the crop of fruit against any would-be raiders!

Ruffed lemur

Is it true?
Tarsiers have a swiveling head.

YES. Tarsiers can turn their head half a full circle, like an owl. This is a perfect way to catch an unsuspecting katydid or other flying insect.

Baby orang-utan

Do monkeys and apes eat bananas?

Primates do eat bananas and even peel them first. Fruit, seeds, flowers, shoots, leaves and fungi (types of mushroom) are all perfect primate meals. The orang-utan's favorite snack is the stinky durian fruit, which smells like cheese.

Which primates eat poison?

Lorises eat insects that are so toxic (poisonous) that they would give other animals a heart attack! They sneak up on their prey and grab it with their hands. The golden bamboo lemur even eats young bamboo shoots that contain cyanide, which is a very dangerous poison.

Amazing! Primates chew gum. Many primates, especially marmosets and bushbabies, scrape away the bark of a gum tree to get at the sap. But when it's fresh the gum is liquid, so the animals drink rather than chew.

Slow loris

235

How do lemur babies get around?

Like all primates, newborn lemur babies cling to their mom's tum as she moves about the forest. As they get bigger and more curious, they have a piggyback, to get a better view.

Ring-tailed lemur

Is it true?
Only moms look after primate babies.

NO. Baby titis are looked after by dad, and young male baboons often borrow a baby. No older male will attack, in case they harm the baby!

? Do primate babies drink milk?

Primates are mammals – they give birth to live young and feed them milk. Most primates, including humans, usually have one baby at a time, but marmosets usually have twins.

Baby orang-utan

Amazing! Baby gibbons wear bonnets. When it's born, a baby gibbon has a cap of fur on the top of its head. Just like human babies, the rest of the baby gibbon's body is completely bare!

Baby orang-utans

? Why are monkeys so cheeky?

All young monkeys love to play and it's as important as school is for you! This is how they learn the skills they will need when they grow up.

Weasel lemur

? What likes to be by itself?

Most primates live in noisy groups, but there are a few loners. The weasel lemur spends most of its life on its own, although it checks on its neighbors by shouting across the forest. The orang-utan prefers to live on its own also, in the dense jungles of Borneo and Sumatra.

 Amazing! Primates have temper tantrums. When a monkey feels cross it sometimes shakes a tree to let off steam, instead of getting angry with the other monkeys, and falling out with its group.

Patas monkeys

Who commands the troop?

The patas monkey is sometimes known as the military monkey. A male leads each group, and makes sure that the 20 females and young are orderly and well-behaved.

Why do primates pick on each other?

Primates often spend much of the day picking through each other's fur. They are looking for tiny biting pests such as ticks, fleas, lice and mites, but grooming is also a way to share smells and bond with each other.

Is it true?
Lemurs drop stink bombs.

YES. Ring-tailed lemur males have stink fights at the borders of their home range. They load their tail with strong-smelling scent and then swish the smell at their rival!

Chimpanzees

Amazing! Monkeys do sentry duty. When a troop is enjoying a feast, one or two animals keep a lookout for predators. They have many different warning calls. For example, they make a certain noise only if a leopard is nearby.

Which is the noisiest primate?

The howler monkey is well-named, because it makes a terrific noise that can be heard up to three miles away through the trees. They hold howling competitions with neighboring groups, to remind each other to keep to their own part of the forest.

Howler monkeys

? Who grins with fright?

Chimpanzees have a special fear grin. They use it to warn others of danger without making a giveaway noise. Sometimes, when chimps come face to face with a predator, they use the horrible grin to try to frighten it away.

Is it true?

Bushbabies rub pee on their feet!

YES. And they also rub pee on their hands! It's their way of leaving lots of smelly graffiti on the trees. Every place they've gripped has a scent which says 'we were here'.

Bushbaby

Mandrill

? Whose backside has something to say?

Many primates have brightly-colored backsides which are easy to see in the dim forest light. These backsides tell other members of their own kind where they are. The mandrill's backsides is the most colorful -- it's bright blue and red!

Who's the king of the swingers?

Gibbons are the champion swingers. They have special bones in their wrists and shoulders to give them plenty of swing as they move from tree to tree. These long-armed apes live in the tropical forests of Malaysia and Indonesia.

Amazing!

Primates have their own cushions. Many primates, including baboons which spend a lot of time sitting around, have built-in padding on their bottoms.

Spider monkey

Who hangs by the tail?

Woolly monkeys, spider monkeys and howler monkeys all have a bare patch of tail for extra grip. They are the only primates that can support all their weight with the tail and hang upside-down.

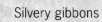
Silvery gibbons

Lemur

Is it true?
Slow lorises really do move slowly.

YES. Lorises are the most relaxed primates. Unlike their busy monkey cousins, lorises stroll very slowly through the forest in search of food.

 ## When are two legs better than four?

Crossing open ground can be a dangerous business with predators about. Lemurs can travel much more quickly on two legs than four. Standing upright also gives them a better view, and frees up their front legs, to pick up food.

Amazing! Chimps take medicine. Chimpanzees sometimes eat plants that don't taste very nice at all, as cures for illness. One herbal remedy is aspilia, which gets rid of stomach ache and worms.

Gorilla painting

Which ape uses tools?

Chimps are very clever, and even make simple tools. They sometimes strip a stick of its bark to make a kind of fishing rod that they use to fish for termites. They also use sticks to gather honey so they needn't get too close to the nest and risk a nasty bee sting!

Termite mound

Can apes paint?

Tame chimps and gorillas have been given paints and paper so they can make pictures. Some of the results look like the work of human artists, and tricked a few of the so-called experts who couldn't tell the difference!

Is it true?
Chimps can talk.

NO. People have taught chimps to point at symbols and to use sign language, so we know that they are clever enough to understand language. But chimps' vocal cords are unable to produce spoken words like ours.

Who carries a pet stone?

Chimpanzees who live on Mount Tai, in West Africa use a stone as a nutcracker to smash open the hard shells of the coula nut. There aren't many rocks on the mountain, so each chimp carries around its own favorite stone.

Chimpanzee

Which monkeys climb trees for cash?

In Sumatra, macaques are used to harvest coconuts. They race to the top of the palm and shake off the fruit for money. The monkeys don't keep the cash, but their owners do! Each year, there are competitions to see who are faster, human or monkey coconut-pickers. Of course, the monkeys usually win!

Pig-tailed macaque

Is it true?
Monkeys and music go together.

YES. Or at least, they used to. Over 100 years ago street performers called organ-grinders used to travel from town to town with their barrel organs. They used cute capuchin monkeys to collect money from the audience.

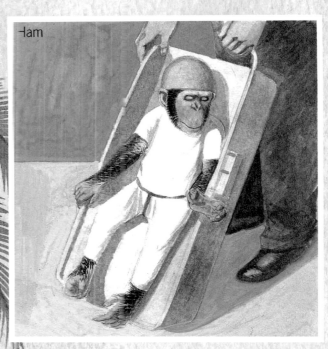

Ham

Can apes survive in space?

In 1961, a chimp called Ham was sent into space and survived the 16-minute flight. Ham paved the way for people to travel to space.

Capuchin monkey

Which monkeys use computers?

Capuchin monkeys are so clever and easy to train that some have been taught to do all sorts of tasks, including using computers! These helper monkeys live with disabled owners

 Amazing! The pharaohs of ancient Egypt often kept primate pets. The animals had their own servants and were lavished with gifts. Still, their favorites would have been big bowls of fruit, not glittering jewels!

Emperor tamarin

 Amazing! Some people think that there are primates yet to be discovered – abominable snowmen! There are many tales of monstrous primates in remote parts of the world, including the yeti from central Asia.

Golden lion tamarin

? Should people keep primates in zoos?

Primates are happiest in the wild, but zoos do important work. They breed animals that are becoming endangered, such as the golden lion tamarin or the silvery marmoset. Zoos also help people to learn about their ape and monkey cousins. This helps people to understand better why primates should be protected in the wild.

Why are primates in danger?

Not all primates are threatened, but some are. Some, such as the emperor tamarin with its beautiful whiskery moustache, are caught to be sold as pets. Gorillas and orang-utans are in danger because people are destroying their habitat and are also hunting them. There are only about 650 gorillas left in the wild.

Is it true?
People eat chimp and chips.

NO. A few apes and monkeys are caught for food, but the biggest threats are the pet trade and the destruction of the places where they live.

Bamboo lemur

Which primate came back from the dead?

Sometimes primates are thought to be extinct, only to re-appear. This happened with the greater bamboo lemur. Most primates are shy and good at hiding. Also, they often live in remote places which are difficult to explore.

Glossary

Abdomen The back part of an insect or arachnid's body.

Air bladder An air-filled sac that helps keep fish afloat. Sharks do not have an air bladder, but have a huge oily liver instead.

Antennae A pair of 'feelers' on the head, which help an animal taste, smell and touch.

Anti-freeze A chemical which prevents water, blood and other liquids from freezing solid.

Ape A tailless primate; a gorilla, orang-utan, chimp, bonobo, gibbon or siamang.

Arachnid Member of the group of animals which includes spiders, scorpions and mites.

Baleen Long, tough bristles hanging down inside some whales' mouths. They are used for sieving food from the sea. Only great whales, such as the blue whale have baleen.

Barnacles Tiny shellfish which grow on rocks and the bottom of ships. Barnacles also stick to whales' backs.

Bear Family of carnivores including brown bears, polar bears and grizzly bears.

Blowhole The hole on top of a whale's head which it uses for breathing out.

Blubber A thick layer of fat under a sea mammal's skin, which protects it from the cold.

Camouflage A special coloring or pattern on the surface of an animal, which makes it blend in with its background, making it difficult to see, and less likely to be attacked by another animal.

Canines The pointy teeth in a carnivore's jaw, used for tearing into flesh.

Carnivore Any mammal, or other animal, which has teeth adapted for eating meat.

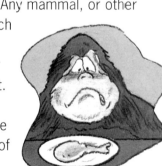

Carrion The dead body of an animal.

Cartilage A rubbery, flexible material. The skeletons of sharks, rays and skate are made of cartilage.

Cat Family of carnivores divided into big cats that roar (lions, tigers, jaguars and leopards) and small cats that purr.

Cold-blooded Animals which cannot control their own body temperature. Instead, they have to rely on the weather to warm them up or cool them down.

Colony A large group of animals living together. Honeybees, ants, termites and some birds all live in colonies.

Cretaceous period The third period in dinosaur history, which lasted from 135 million years ago until the extinction of the dinosaurs about 65 million years ago.

Denticle The sharp points on a shark's skin.

Dog Family of carnivores including wolves, foxes and jackals.

Echo-location The way that some animals use sound to locate food and find their way around. They make sounds which hit solid objects and send back echoes. From these, the animals can tell what the objects are, and where they are.

Embryo A stage in development after an egg is fertilized until the young animal is born or hatches.

Endangered At risk of dying out.

Evolution A gradual change in form over many generations.

Extinct No longer alive anywhere on Earth.

Falconer Someone who breeds and trains falcons and hawks.

Fangs Special teeth through which snakes squirt poison into their enemies or prey.

Flock A large group of birds.

Fossil The preserved remains of something that was once alive.

Genes Special instructions inside every cell of a living being, which tell it how to grow.

Gills Breathing slits behind the head of a fish, used to extract oxygen from water.

Gizzard A special second stomach that birds have, with strong muscles to help grind up and digest food.

Grooming Cleaning the fur of ticks and fleas. Primates often do this for each other.

Habitat The type of place where an animal lives in the wild. The polar bear's habitat is the icy Arctic.

Helper monkey A monkey which has been bred and trained to help and live with a disabled owner.

Hibernation A deep sleep-like state

which many warm and cold-blooded animals go into to survive through the winter.

Ichthyosaurs Marine reptiles that were alive in dinosaur times.

Insect Small animal with three body parts – the head, thorax and abdomen – and three pairs of legs.

Jurassic period The second period in dinosaur history, which lasted from 200 to 135 million years ago.

Krill Tiny, shrimp-like sea creatures. Huge amounts of krill are eaten by whales.

Larva The young stage of a hatched insect, which looks different from the adult.

Lethal Deadly, or fatal.

Litter Baby animals born from the same mother at the same time.

Lobtailing When whales slap their tails on the surface of the sea, as a signal to other whales.

Mammal A warm-blooded animal covered in fur which gives birth to live young and feeds its babies on mother's milk.

Maori The name for the native people of New Zealand and their language.

Marsupial A mammal that gives birth to very undeveloped live young, that live at first in their mother's pouch.

Meteorite A rock which flies through outer space until it lands on Earth, sometimes with disastrous results.

Migrate To move from one place to another, often far away. Birds and animals may migrate to find warmer places to live each winter, or to find more food.

Mimicry
When an animal or bird copies another. Some parrots and mynah birds can even mimic the sound of the telephone.

Monkey Usually a primate with a tail although not all monkeys have tails.

Nectar Sugary liquid produced by plants, and collected by insects. Honeybees use nectar to make honey.

Paleontologist A person who studies fossilized remains.

Paralyze To make an animal helpless so that it cannot move.

Parasite A tiny animal that lives in or on another animal from which it gets its food. Parasites are often harmful to their 'host'.

Pedigree A domestic (not wild) animal that has been bred to have certain characteristics.

Plankton Tiny animals and plants that float in the sea. Some of the larger sharks and several types of whales feed only on plankton which they filter from the water.

Plesiosaurs Marine reptiles with large flippers, which were alive in dinosaur times.

Pods The name for family groups of dolphins, seals and whales.

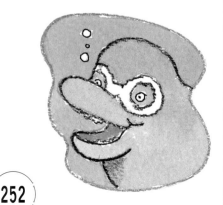

Predator An animal which hunts other animals for food.

Preening When a bird combs and tidies its feathers with its beak.

Prey An animal which is hunted by another animal for food.

Pride A group of lions who live together.

Primate A group of big-brained mammals, with forward facing eyes, made up of six different groups: lemurs; lorises and galagos; tarsiers; New World monkeys; Old World monkeys; and apes and humans.

Pterosaurs Reptiles which traveled through the air in prehistoric times.

Pupa A larva enters the pupa stage before turning into an adult insect. A butterfly pupa is called a chrysalis.

Rainforest An evergreen tropical forest where there is heavy rainfall most days.

Saltwater crocodile Also known as the Estuarine crocodile, they are the largest crocodiles, and can also live in fresh water.

Sauropods Large plant-eating dinosaurs that included Diplodocus.

School A large number of the same kind of fish all swimming together. Hammerhead sharks swim in schools.

Talons Long, curved claws. Birds of prey use their talons to grip and tear at their prey.

Tendon A strong cord which connects a muscle to a bone.

Territory The patch of land or sea in which an animal lives. Many animals fiercely defend their territory.

Triassic period The first period in dinosaur history, which lasted from 225 to 200 million years ago, when the first of the dinosaurs appeared on Earth.

Venom Poison.

Vertebrates Animals which have a spine inside their bodies. Vertebrates include mammals, birds, reptiles and amphibians.

Index